AROUND THE WORLD·
·ONE BITE AT A TIME
AN INTERNATIONAL COLLECTION OF PARTY FOODS

Rebecca Brown Karavatakis
Lafayette, Louisiana

DEDICATION AND ACKNOWLEDGMENTS

To my three wonderful children, who met me with encouragement and enthusiasm, I dedicate this book that they may always reach beyond the horizons.

Special appreciation I give to my Mom who gave to me, above all else, the gift of sharing with others. For all the hours spent watching and helping her prepare food, Hors d'Oeuvres and fancy desserts, I hope to share these experiences with others.

And to all my family and friends, who gave of themselves in ideas and recipes, this book is written for your enjoyment and sharing.

ON THE COVER

The photo of the Earth was taken by NASA from a satellite 22,300 miles out in space.

The "peligator" was created in June of 1984 near Cypress Lake on the U.S.L. campus. We spotted a pelican sitting atop a tree stump while we were feeding popcorn to alligators in the lake. My son, George, said "you could cross an alligator with a pelican and make a peligator." Jaque made his first appearance on the noon show at KLFY-TV in October, 1984, as the mascot for the Ascension Day School Haunted House.

The cover design and lettering idea came from my son, Pete, who, along with his computer, was always ready to help.

PREFACE

This book is intended only as a beginning, or introduction to the fascinating art of entertaining with food. Whether a simple theme or an international affair the entire production is individually yours.

When it comes to planning a large party, the public Library is the place to start. Without a large investment in special books you can access books on garnishes, table settings and room decorations as well as the best variety of special cookbooks available.

No matter what your occasion, you will almost always have at least one guest who is on a special diet — if you know about it in advance, something simple can be prepared. However, with a large party, having an area prepared makes these people feel welcome and most folks will enjoy nibbling such goodies. Raw vegetables, cut into decorative shapes and small fruit pieces, such as grapes and strawberries are excellent. Micro-crisp vegetables served on picks decorating a styrofoam cone draped with curly edge parsley makes a beautiful and healthy centerpiece. Both regular and "lite" dressings or dips can be served.

Most people are so concerned about what brands of liquor to buy that they often forget about the guests who do not drink. The proper beverage assortment should include several bottles of non-alcoholic "wines" as well as at least one sugar free and one caffeine free drink.

Fillers have their place at large parties. A block of cream cheese, sprinkled with fine chopped nuts or parsley and covered with a thick spicy sauce can be easily served with crackers or celery sticks. Seasoned, toasted nuts and cereals are nice to place near the area of the bar. Chips and dips should be reserved for more casual settings.

Miniature hamburgers, corn dogs and the like are perfect for parties for little people. Also it's a nice treat to plan an after party for the kids the day after your own party. The leftovers make a great hit and the kids enjoy having their own special time, especially at holidays.

Never, never be afraid to try something new! If you have a favorite dish at your house, chances are it can be made suitable for serving — One Bite at a Time...

TABLE OF CONTENTS

And our journey begins —

"One Bite at a Time"...

Note: Full pages by the same person are acknowledged only at the bottom.

PICKLES/RELISHES

CUCUMBER RINGS
MOCK CRABAPPLES

*2 gal. oversized cucumbers
sliced ¼" thick
2 c. lime
8½ qts. water
1 T. alum
10 c. sugar
1 c. vinegar*

*2 c. vinegar
1 sm. bottle red food
coloring
2 c. water
8 broken cinnamon sticks
6-oz. pkg. red hots candy*

Remove seeds, leaving a round hole in center of each slice. Mix lime with 8½ quarts water. Pour over rings and soak 24 hours.(DO NOT soak in aluminum.) Drain and rinse; simmer in mixture of 1 cup vinegar, red food coloring, alum, and enough water to cover, for 2 hours. Drain and place in large container. Make a syrup of 2 cups vinegar, 2 cups water, 10 cups sugar, 8 broken cinnamon sticks and 6-oz. red hots candy. Bring to boil and pour over rings; let stand over-night. Next day, drain and reheat syrup and pour over rings. Let stand overnight. Next day pack cucumber rings in jars. Reheat syrup to boiling and pour over rings. Seal at once.

Variation: Omit red coloring and red hots candy; add green coloring, mint and cloves.

Yield: 8 pints

*Irma Roesler Beisel
Leawood, Kansas*

GERTRUDE'S CUCUMBERS

1 qt. sm. cucumbers, peeled
 and sliced ⅛'' thick
1 pt. pearl onions
½ c. mayonnaise

Sweet pickle juice
Tony's seasoning
Dash salt & pepper

Remove first skin from onions. Place in large bowl with cucumbers. Combine ½ c. mayonnaise, pickle juice enough to thin to consistancy of cream. Add salt, pepper and Tony's seasoning, to taste. Pour over cucumbers mixture; cover tightly and refrigerate at least 2 hours. Lightly drain and serve with toothpicks.

Yield: 1½ quarts

Gertrude Roesler Brown
Sunset, La.

CRISP-AS-ICE CUCUMBER SLICES

½ c. salt
4 qts. thinly sliced cucumbers
8 onions, thinly sliced
2 green peppers, cut in strips
4 c. sugar

1½ t. tumeric
½ t. cloves
3½ t. mustard seeds
4½ c. vinegar

Sprinkle salt over the cucumbers and mix together. Empty a tray of ice cubes in center of cucumbers. Let stand three hours. Combine sugar, spices and vinegar; heat to boiling. Drain cucumbers thoroughly. Pour hot syrup over them; heat over low temperature to scalding. Do not allow mixture to boil. Stir frequently to prevent scorching. Ladle into hot, sterilized jars and seal at once. Process in boiling water bath (212° F) for 5 minutes.

Yield: 5½ pts.

Thelma Moser
Gretna, La.

CHINESE CELERY

2 green onions, w/tops minced
2 t. white pepper
2 T. sesame oil
1 T. ginger, minced

2 stalks celery, trimmed
¼ c. soy sauce
1 T. rice vinegar
2 t. sugar (or "Equal")

Cut celery to strips, about 3" long. Heat pot of water to boiling and blanch celery for about 30 seconds. Drain; rinse until cold and drain again. Combine pepper, soy sauce, onions, vinegar, ginger and sugar in bowl and stir until sugar is dissolved. Pour over celery; chill.

Yield: 5 to 6 dozen

DILLY MIX

2 pkg. frozen Brussel sprouts
1 pt. pearl onions
8-oz. fresh mushrooms

1 pt. Italian dressing
1 t. dill weed
2 T. dried chives

Cook Brussel sprouts and drain. Cool 10 minutes. Wash mushrooms and cut in half with stems on. Remove outer skin on onions. Combine vegetables in gallon size Zip-loc bag. Mix other ingredients together and pour over vegetables. Remove air from bag and seal. Refrigerate overnight. Drain and serve.

Yield: 2½ pints

Becky Karavatakis
Lafayette, La.

PICKLED MUSHROOMS

1 lb. fresh mushrooms
3-oz. olive oil
¼ c. rice vinegar
1 t. dry mustard
1 t. salt

1 bay leaf
5 whole peppercorns
1 toe garlic, minced
1 t. honey

Clean and trim stems from mushrooms. Put mushroom caps in pot and add enough water to cover. Add a dash of salt and bring water to boil. Reduce heat and boil gently until mushrooms no longer float. Drain and pack into hot sterile jars. Combine remaining ingredients and bring to boil. Reduce heat and simmer 5 minutes. Pour over mushrooms and seal tightly. Cool completely and store in refrigerator.

Yield: 1 pint

PICKLED SHRIMP

1 lb. shrimp, (41-45/lb.)
1 T. pickling spices
1 T. Creole mustard
1 t. horseradish
¼ c. olive oil

½ t. garlic salt
¼ t. celery salt
½ c. apple cider vinegar
2 scallions w/tops, sliced

Peel shrimp, leaving tail of shell only to first joint. Put shrimp and pickling spices in 2 quart sauce pan. Cover shrimp with water. Bring to boil; reduce to medium heat and cook for 2 minutes. Strain water, leaving spices with shrimp. Place in serving dish. Combine mustard, horseradish, oil, salts, vinegar and onions. Pour over shrimp. Cover and refrigerate overnight. Serve cold.

Yield: about 3½ dozen

Becky Karavatakis
Lafayette, La.

MARINATED FISH

2 lbs. fillet of mackerel
 or other firm fish
1 c. lemon juice
2 lg. tomatoes, peeled
 seeded, chopped fine
1 lg. yellow onion,
 minced
½ c. olive oil
2 med. avocados, peeled,
 pitted, diced

2½ oz. jar capers,
 drained and split
12 pimiento-stuffed
 olives, chopped
¼ t. coriander
1 yellow banana pepper,
 seeded, minced
Lemon wedges
Salt and white pepper
Parsley

Cut fish into ½" pieces. Place in Zip-loc bag; pour lemon juice over fish. Remove air from bag and seal. Refrigerate one hour. Drain; discard juice. Combine fish, tomatoes, onion, oil, capers, olives and coriander in mixing bowl. Drizzle juice of several lemon wedges over avocado and add to mixture; toss lightly. Season with salt and pepper. Refrigerate until ready to serve. Garnish top with banana peppers and parsley.

Yield: 5 to 6 doz. pieces

MARINATED OLIVES

2 c. pimiento-stuffed olives
2 c. Kalamata olives
2 t. dried oregano
1 t. dried mint
1 t. dill weed

Juice of 2 lemons
¾ c. olive oil
⅓ c. fresh parsley, chopped
1 clove garlic, minced
1 t. black pepper

Combine ingredients; cover and refrigerate overnight.

Yield: 2 pints

*Becky Karavatakis
Lafayette, La.*

FRESH GREEK OLIVES

1st 30 days
Olives
Water

Rinse olives and put in container. Cover with water. Rest 3 to 4 days. Rinse. Repeat prior steps for 30 days.

<u>2nd 30 days</u>
Olives   Water
Salt   Raw egg

   Drain olives and put in container. Put enough water to cover olives in mixing container. Add 1 raw egg in shell. Add enough salt for egg to float leaving circle about the size of a penny. Remove egg. Pour salt water brine over olives. Cover container and let set for 30 days.

<u>Final Preparation</u>
Olives   Vinegar
Water   Olive oil

Rinse olives two times. Place olives in container. In mixing container combine 2 parts vinegar, 1 part water and 5 parts olive oil. Pour over olives. Cover tightly and let set for at least two weeks.

Yield: Varies   *Nick Karavatakis*
                                                            Mantamados, Greece

PICKLED QUAIL EGGS

1 c. white vinegar
1 T. pickling spice
60 hard boiled quail eggs

3 c. water
1 med. onion, minced

Combine all except eggs, and bring to a boil. Reduce heat to medium and cook 2 minutes. Strain and reserve. Shell eggs and put into sterilized jars. Reheat brine to boiling and pour over to cover. Process 10 minutes in hot water bath or seal with lids and store in refrigerator until ready to use.

Note: to remove shells easier: cover eggs with water and about 1 cup vinegar. Let stand one hour, drain and peel.

Yield: 3 to 4 pints

Becky Karavatakis
Lafayette, La.

TOURSI
VEGETABLES IN BRINE

Brine
Whole small green tomatoes
Celery sticks, cut 2 to 3″
Cauliflower, cut into flowerettes
Green peppers, cut in strips
   about ½″ wide

Per quart jar:
vinegar
2 cloves garlic
1 t. mixed whole spice
1 sprig fresh dill or
½ t. dill weed

To make brine, insert a raw egg, in shell, in water, and add enough salt for egg to float leaving a circle about the size of a penny. Wash all vegetables and place into quart jars. Fill with brine and seal tightly. Shake and turn jars every other day for 10 days. Discard brine. Fill jars to 1″ from top with vinegar. Add garlic, spices and dill to each jar. Let set 2 to 3 weeks, shaking every 4 to 5 days.

Yield: Varies

Ted Karavatakis
Lafayette, La.

MARINATED VEGETABLE PLATTER

Vegetables
½ lb. carrots
2 sm. zucchini
½ lb. fresh mushrooms

1 bunch broccoli buds
3 sm. yellow squash
1 can artichoke hearts,
quartered

Marinade
1¼ c. olive oil
1¼ c. red wine vinegar
1 t. garlic powder
1 t. Tony's seasoning

1 t. dry mustard
1 t. sugar
1 t. Italian seasoning

Place vegetables in separate containers. Combine marinade ingredients. Divide and pour over vegetables and refrigerate overnight. Drain and arrange on platter.

Yield: Vegetables for 16'' platter
about 2½ cups marinade

PIZZA POPCORN

⅓ c. butter
8 c. popped corn
¼ t. chili powder

1 t. Italian seasoning
2 T. parmesan cheese,
grated

Melt butter and seasoning; stir in cheese. Pour over popcorn. Mix well.

Yield: 8 cups

Becky Karavatakis
Lafayette, La.

SPICED CASHEWS

3 c. raw cashews
2 T. butter
¼ c. honey

½ t. cinnamon
½ t. ginger
¼ t. nutmeg

Melt butter in cast iron skillet over low heat. Stir in honey, cinnamon, ginger and nutmeg. Bring to boil. Stir in cashews and reduce to medium heat. Cook about 15 minutes, stirring often. Turn out on cookie sheet and cool completely. Store in airtight container.

Yield: 3 cups

BAYOU PECANS

3 c. pecan halves
3 T. butter
Dash Tabasco sauce

1½ t. Tony's seasoning
2 t. Worcestershire sauce

Melt butter in roasting pan. Combine Tabasco, Tony's and Worcestershire; stir into butter. Add pecans; stir to coat, and toast at 300° F. for about 30 minutes.

Yield: 3 cups

Becky Karavatakis
Lafayette, La.

FRUIT NIBBLERS

4 c. rolled oats
1 c. dried banana slices
1 c. broken walnuts and pecans
½ c. toasted sesame seeds
⅓ c. sunflower oil

¼ c. honey
½ c. raisins
½ c. chopped dried apricots
½ c. chopped dried peaches
½ c. chopped dried apples

Mix oats, nuts, sesame seeds, oil, and honey together well. Preheat oven to 400° F. Spread in large roasting pan. Bake about 15 minutes or until lightly browned on edges, stirring every 3 minutes. Cool completely. Stir in fruit. Store in airtight containers.

Yield: about 2 quarts

WATERMELON PICKLES

2 lbs. thick watermelon rind
4 c. sugar
1½ c. vinegar
2 T. pickling spices

1 stick cinnamon, broken
1 oz. lime
1 gal. water
Optional: 1 jalapeno/pt.

Trim all red and green from rind. Cut into chunks and put into large non-aluminum container. Dissolve lime in water; pour over rind, and soak overnight. Rinse lightly and drain. Combine sugar, vinegar, pickling spices and cinnamon; bring to a boil, stirring until sugar is dissolved. Pour over rind; bring to boil and reduce to simmer for one hour. Pour into sterile jars and seal. If desired, add one jalapeno, split to each jar just prior to sealing.

Yield: about 4 pints

Becky Karavatakis
Lafayette, La.

CRUN-CHEWY FRUIT MIX

2 lg. apples
2 lg. bananas
2 lg. pears

1 lg. can pineapple chunks
packed in own juice
Juice of 1 lemon

Drain juice from pineapple and combine with lemon juice in shallow bowl. Peel and core apples and pears, one at a time and soak in pineapple-lemon juice for two minutes. Drain and repeat with remaining apples and pears. Peel and slice bananas ⅛″ thick and soak in pineapple-lemon juice for two minutes. Spray mesh cake racks with non-stick spray. Place fruit on racks in single layer and place in oven at 150° F. Apples and pineapples should be pliable and ready to remove in about 24 hours. Pears should be pliable and slightly leathery in 24 hours. The bananas should be crispy (after cooling 10 to 15 minutes) after 28 to 30 hours. Let cool completely and store in air tight containers.

Note: smaller pieces dry faster than larger pieces, so you may have to adjust your time. Also, finished product will be reduced to about ⅓ starting quantity.

Yield: Varies

GRANOLA MIX

5 c. rolled oats
½ c. wheat germ
1 c. dried Crun-chewy Mix
1 c. raisins

½ c. brown sugar
½ c. raw honey
1 t. vanilla
1 t. cinnamon

Mix together well to distribute fruit evenly. Spread out on baking racks lined with paper towels. Dry in oven at 150° F. until crispy; let cool and store in airtight containers.

Yield: about 2 quarts

Becky Karavatakis
Lafayette, La.

SAUCES/JELLIES

PICANTE SAUCE

4 c. tomatoes   4 jalapeno peppers
1 med. onion   2 cloves garlic
1 bell pepper

Process; and Add:

4 t. vinegar   1 t. sugar
2½ t. salt

Cook until mixture is thick enough for taste. Pour into sterile jars and seal.

Yield: about 1 pint   *Juanita Todd*
                                               Needville, Texas

SEAFOOD COCKTAIL SAUCE

12 oz. bottle Heinz chili sauce   1 t. lemon juice
1 T. horseradish   1 T. Worcestershire
½ t. or more Tabasco   Salt and pepper, to taste

Combine and chill at least one hour. Makes about 1½ cups.

Variations: 1) add ¼ c. fine minced onions; 2) add ¼ t. garlic puree and 1 T. onion puree; 3) omit horseradish and add 2 T. Creole mustard.

Yield: about 1½ cups   *Becky Karavatakis*
                                               Lafayette, La.

HOT MUSTARD

⅔ c. rice vinegar
4-oz. dry mustard

3 lg. eggs
1 c. sugar

Combine and cook in double boiler until thickened. Refrigerate until ready to serve.

Yield: about 2 cups

HOISON DIPPING SAUCE

1 c. sour cream
½ c. Hoison sauce

½ c. chili sauce
Dash Tabasco

Process until smooth; chill. Serve with fresh vegetables.

Yield: 1 cup

SWEET 'N TART GLAZE

6-oz. can frozen limeade, thawed
½ c. honey

¾ c. peanut oil
2 t. poppy seeds

Process only until smooth. Do Not Whip. Pour over fresh cut fruit.

Viaration: Reduce honey to ¼ cup and use 6 oz. can Frozen Concentrated Tropical Fruit mixer, Strawberry Daiquiri or Pina Colada flavor.

Yield: 2 cups

Becky Karavatakis
Lafayette, La.

SWEET 'N SOUR SAUCE

2 1-lb. cans crushed pineapple,
  packed in own juice
¼ c. corn starch
¼ c. brown sugar, packed
1 c. chicken broth
¾ c. rice or white wine
  vinegar

1 T. soy sauce
2 T. ketchup
1 sm. can drained water
  chestnuts, minced
4 green onions, w/tops
  sliced thin
1 lg. bell pepper, minced

Drain pineapple; reserve 1¼ c. juice. Mix cornstarch with brown sugar; heat to boiling in sauce pan with pineapple juice, broth, vinegar, soy, and ketchup. Reduce to medium and stir until thickened. Add green onions and bell peppers; continue to stir for 1 to 2 minutes. Refrigerate, covered.

Yield: 3½ cups

SWEET AND SOUR SAUCE

3 c. ketchup
1½ c. sugar
10.5 oz. can Campbell's tomato soup
1 c. olive oil
1 t. paprika

1 clove garlic, minced
1 t. dry mustard
1 t. Worcestershire sauce
1 t. white pepper
1 t. salt

Combine and process until smooth. Refrigerate, covered.

Yield: about 6½ cups

Becky Karavatakis
Lafayette, La.

REMOULADE SAUCE

¾ c. minced onions

4-oz. jar capers, drained

1 c. fresh chopped parsley

1 T. Creole mustard

1 c. peanut oil

½ c. olive oil

½ t. salt

1 t. black pepper

¼ c. red wine vinegar

Combine ingredients and process lightly. Cover and refrigerate. Use as a marinade or sauce for boiled shrimp, lobster, crawfish, turtle or alligator.

Variation: for Mediterranean Marinade: omit mustard; add a 2¼ oz. can anchovies, drained; 1 t. Italian seasoning; ¼ t. garlic powder; and 2 T. lemon juice.

Yield: 3 cups

Becky Karavatakis
Lafayette, La.

AVGOLEMONO SAUCE
EGG AND LEMON SAUCE

4 lg. eggs

Juice of 2 lemons

1 c. chicken stock

Heat stock. Beat eggs to soft peak stage. Continue beating while slowly adding lemon juice. Stir about ¼ of stock into egg mixture; return entire mixture to sauce pan just to heat through, DO NOT BOIL. Use as marinade or dipping sauce for Dolmadaikia or meatballs.

Yield: about 2½ cups

Helen Karavatakis
Skopelos, Greece

GREEK DRESSING

3½ oz. cider vinegar
½ oz. water
1½ c. olive oil
1 t. dill weed
Salt and pepper, to taste

1 t. Italian seasoning
Dash garlic powder
Dash onion powder
Dash dried mint

Cut vinegar with water. Combine remaining ingredients in covered jar. Shake well before serving. Does not need to be refrigerated.

Yield: 2 cups

Ted Karavatakis
Lafayette, La.

POPPY SEED DRESSING

¾ c. sugar
1 t. dry mustard
½ med. onion, finely
   grated

1 t. salt
¼ c. wesson oil
⅓ c. vinegar
1⅓ t. poppy weeds

Mix sugar, mustard, and salt. Add oil and vinegar beating constantly in blender. Add onion and poppy seed. If dressing separates, shake before serving. Refrigerate until ready to serve. Pour dressing into a cantalope or honeydew melon; surround with melon balls, pineapple chunks, strawberries, and peach chunks.

Yield: about 1 pint

Sharron Brown Mayers
Baton Rouge, La.

AVOCADO/POPPY SEED DRESSING

2 lg. ripe avocados
1 c. orange juice
1 t. poppy seeds

Juice of one lemon
1 T. honey
½ t. salt

Peel and pit avocados. Process avocado with remaining ingredients until smooth. Serve over fresh fruit.

Yield: about 2 cups

CANAPY MAYONNAISE

1 envelope unflavored gelatin
1 c. Hellmann's mayonnaise

¼ c. cold water

Soften gelatin in cold water. Stir over low heat until dissolved. Add to mayonnaise and blend well. Spread or brush a thin layer to form a protective base on bread or crackers.

Yield: 1 ¼ cup

MUFFULETTA SALAD MIX

1 c. pimento-stuffed olives
⅓ c. red wine vinegar
1 t. Italian seasoning

¾ c. olive oil
1 clove garlic, minced
2 ribs celery, chopped

Combine olives, garlic and celery in processor. Process until fine-minced. Stir in remaining ingredients and refrigerate at least 24 hours.

Yield: 2 cups

Becky Karavatakis
Lafayette, La.

RUBY RED PEPPER JAM

6 lg. red bell peppers   1 c. red wine vinegar
1½ t. salt   Tabasco sauce
1½ c. sugar

Sprinkle salt over peppers; let stand, covered, overnight. Drain and place in saucepan with vinegar and sugar. Bring to boil, stir and reduce to simmer. Stir gently and cook until thick like honey. Transfer to hot sterile jars leaving ½" head space and seal with hot lids and rings. Leave jars still overnight. Store in cool dark place at least 2 weeks before using. (Tabasco sauce can be added before cooking or stirred in just before use — this way if "some like it hot, some like it NOT so hot" you have it both ways from one batch.) Pour about ¼ c. over 8 oz. block of cream cheese and serve with crackers.

Yield: about 2 pints   Becky Karavatakis
                                                   Lafayette, La.

HOT PEPPER JELLY

1 c. ground bell pepper   ½ t. salt
¼ c. hot peppers, ground   6 oz. bottle Certo
6½ c. sugar   fruit pectin
1½ c. apple cider vinegar   ½ c. chopped pimento

Mix sugar and vinegar in large kettle. When dissolved, add peppers and salt. Bring to rolling boil. Take off fire and let stand 5 minutes. Add pectin and stir. Pour in hot sterilized jars and seal. To serve, pour over 8 oz. block of cream cheese. Serve with crackers.

                                                 Carol Christie
                                                 Lafayette, La.

CRANBERRY CHUTNEY

2 c. fresh cranberries
1 lg. tomato, peeled, seeded, chopped
½ c. raisins
1 med. onion, chopped
1 t. salt
½ t. white pepper

1 c. packed dark brown sugar
½ c. red wine vinegar
½ t. ground ginger
½ t. ground cloves
¾ c. water

Bring water to boil. Add cranberries, tomatoes, raisins, onion, salt and pepper; return to boil. Reduce heat, and simmer for 15 minutes. Stir in remaining ingredients. Cook over low heat 40 minutes, stirring occasionally. Cool. Cover and refrigerate.

Variation: replace cranberries with fresh apples.

Yield: about 2¾ cups

WATERMELON RIND PRESERVES

1 lb. watermelon rind
1½ c. sugar
½ c. water

2 sticks cinnamon
Juice of ½ lemon
1 t. powdered lime

Peel and cube melon. Put in non-aluminum container with 1 teaspoon of lime dissolved in 1 quart of water. Soak overnight. Drain and rinse 2 to 3 times. Put in saucepan with sugar, honey, water and cinnamon sticks. Bring to boil and simmer for one hour. Stir from time to time and skim off top as it accumulates. Stir in lemon juice at end of cooking. Place in sterile pint jars and seal.

Yield: about 2 pints

Becky Karavatakis
Lafayette, La.

"STRAWBERRIED" FIGS

2 c. peeled figs
½ pkg. strawberry jello

½ c. sugar
1 T. lemon juice

Microwave figs in 3 quart dish for 2 minutes. Stir in dry jello and cook 2 minutes longer. Add sugar and lemon juice. Cook 6 minutes; stirring after each 2 minutes. Pour into hot sterile jar and seal with paraffin.

Yield: 1 pint

Gertrude Roesler Brown
Sunset, La.

PEACH CONSERVE

2 c. chopped peaches
8 oz. bottle maraschino
  cherries, chopped
Juice from cherries

20 oz. can crushed, pineapple,
  drained
7½ c. sugar
6 oz. bottle liquid fruit pectin

Combine peaches, pineapple, cherries, and juice in a 4-quart casserole dish. Microwave, covered for 10 minutes on high. Stir in sugar. Cook, uncovered, 15 minutes; stirring every 5 minutes (mixture should be boiling). Stir in pectin. Cool 10 to 15 minutes longer to 228° F. Stir 5 minutes to cool slightly. Pour into sterile jars. Seal with paraffin.

Yield: 5 12 oz. jars

Sharron Brown Mayers
Baton Rouge, La.

SOUPS/SALADS

ICED CRAB SOUP

3 red onions, minced fine
1 lb. cucumbers (2-3)
½ c. celery, minced fine
3 T. butter
2 lg. tomatoes, peeled,
   seeded, and chopped fine
5 c. fish stock

1 ½ c. white crab meat,
   picked and flaked
2 T. parsley, minced
3 green onion tops,
   thin sliced
1 t. mint, minced

To make stock: put 2 cups fish, 1 chopped onion, and ½ teaspoon salt, in cheese cloth. Add 6 cups water and 2 tablespoons lemon juice. Boil about 5 minutes; reduce to simmer, cover, and cook for 20 minutes. Strain and reserve. Saute onions and cucumbers in butter until clear. Add tomatoes and simmer five minutes. Stir in stock and bring to a boil. Reduce heat; cover, and simmer 20 minutes. Let cool. Puree in blender about 2 cups at a time. Combine mixture in large bowl with crab, parsley, onion tops, mint, salt and pepper. Chill 3 to 4 hours or overnight. Position serving bowl in dish of crushed ice and serve from small soup cups.

Yield: about 7 cups

CHILLED AVOCADO SOUP

1 lg. ripe avocado, peeled,
   pitted and diced
1 c. chicken broth
1 tomato, peeled and minced

1 sm. onion, minced
2 t. lime juice
1 c. Half and Half
Salt and pepper, to taste

Process all except tomato until smooth. Chill at least 1 hour. Serve in small cups or brandy snifters. Garnish tops with minced tomatoes.

Yield: 12 4-oz. servings

Becky Karavatakis
Lafayette, La.

CREAM OF ARTICHOKE SOUP

1 10-oz. pkg. frozen artichoke hearts	2 c. Half and Half cream
1½ c. chicken broth	1 ripe avocado
1 T. lemon juice	Salt and Tabasco, to taste

Pit and dice avocado. Sprinkle with lemon juice. Reserve. Simmer artichoke hearts in chicken broth 15 to 20 minutes. Drain, reserving broth and process with cream until smooth. Return to chicken broth; add salt and Tabasco, to taste. Heat through, do not boil. Chill at least one hour and serve cold. Garnish with diced avocado pieces.

Yield: 1 qt. or 8 4-oz. servings

GAZPACHO

1 lg. peeled, ripe tomato	1 t. paprika
1 lg. peeled, seeded cucumber	1 t. sweet basil
2 toes garlic, minced	1 t. honey
1 sm. bell pepper, chunked	½ t. cumin
1 yellow onion, diced	½ t. Tony's seasoning
½ chicken broth	2 T. olive oil

Reserve:

1 lg. ripe tomato, peeled, chopped fine	1 lg. cucumber, peeled chopped fine
2½ c. chicken broth	

Process or blend to near smooth all but the reserve ingredients. Add reserve ingredients; blend. Chill. Serve from iced punch bowl in small brandy glasses.

Yield: about 6 cups

Becky Karavatakis
Lafayette, La.

ROQUEFORT VICHYSSOISE

1 lg. yellow onion,
  chopped fine
¼ c. unsalted butter
1 qt. chicken stock
4-oz. Roquefort cheese,
  finely crumbled

¼ t. salt
Dash white pepper
2 c. buttermilk
2 T. green onion tops,
  chopped fine
2 c. potatoes, peeled
  and diced small

Saute onions in butter until clear. Stir in stock, potatoes, salt and pepper. Heat to boiling; reduce heat and simmer 20 minutes. Puree soup about 3 cups at a time until smooth. Refrigerate, covered, at least 4 hours. Stir in buttermilk, salt and pepper. Ladle into cups and sprinkle tops with cheese and onion tops.

Yield: about 12 4-oz. cups

CURRIED CRANBERRY SOUP

2 qts. chicken stock
4 c. cranberries
1 lg. onion, minced
½ c. sugar
1 qt. Half and Half cream

1 T. curry powder
2 t. salt
Dash Tabasco sauce
Juice of one lemon
2 T. cornstarch

Heat to boil stock, cranberries, onion and sugar. Stir and reduce heat. Simmer for 10 minutes. Mix cream, cornstarch, salt and Tabasco until smooth. Stir into cranberry mixture and simmer 10 minutes, stirring often, DO NOT BOIL. Remove from heat and stir in lemon juice. Puree about 3 cups at a time. Cover, and refrigerate. Serve chilled in champagne glasses. Garnish with sprig of mint.

Yield: about 3½ quarts
about 50 3½-oz. cups

Becky Karavatakis
Lafayette, La.

CHICKEN AND POTATO SALAD KIEV

3 c. boned chicken breasts,
   diced very small
3 ribs celery, chopped fine
1 lb. red potatoes, boiled
   and diced very small
1 t. dill weed

3 lg. hard boiled eggs
6 green onions w/tops,
   chopped fine
1 4" dill pickle, chopped
   into small pieces
Sour Cream Dressing

Combine all ingredients and mix with ½ batch of Sour Cream Dressing. Chill for 1 to 2 hours to set flavors. Form into desired shape on bed of lettuce and pour remaining dressing over top.

Variation: This is also good made with shrimp or crawfish, to which you must add a dash or two of Tabasco. Very good as a stuffing for cherry tomatoes or celery sticks.

Sour Cream Dressing

¾ c. mayonnaise
¾ c. sour cream
1½ t. dill weed
1 t. white vinegar

2 oz. jar capers, drained
¼ t. white pepper
¼ t. salt

Process or blend until smooth. Chill remaining dressing before pouring over salad. Makes about 1¾ cups.

Yield: about 2 quarts

Becky Karavatakis
Lafayette, La.

CHICKEN SALAD

1 c. cooked chicken, diced
¼ c. mayonnaise
1 med. onion, minced
¼ t. dill weed

3 ribs celery, diced
2 T. sweet pickle relish
2-3 dashes Tabasco
¼ t. salt

Process or blend to fine minced consistency. Mound on a bed of curly leaf lettuce. Garnish as desired and serve with crackers or celery sticks.

Variations: 1) add ½ med. bell pepper, diced and 1 canned pimento, cut into pieces. This makes about 1½ cups. 2) omit dill weed and sweet pickle relish. use ½ c. mayonnaise, and add 1 t. curry powder and ½ c. toasted almonds. This makes about 1⅔ cups.

Yield: about 1¼ cups

QUAIL SALAD

2 quail, boiled, boned and diced
1 T. sweet pickle relish
1 t. Creole mustard
4 sliced crisp crumbled
   bacon

1 lg. egg, boiled, and chopped
2 T. mayonnaise
2 T. green onion tops, minced
¼ t. salt
2-3 dashes Tabasco

Combine all ingredients. Chill and serve in mound on lettuce leaves. Sprinkle top with parsley and paprika as desired. Garnish with cherry tomatoes. Serve with crackers.

Variation: Quail spread: mince quail; double mayonnaise.

Yield: about 2 cups

Becky Karavatakis
Lafayette, La.

SHARRON'S SHRIMP SALAD

3 lb. shrimp
3 lg. eggs, hard boiled
  chopped fine
3 T. dill pickles,
  chopped fine
4-5 heaping T. mayonnaise
1 lg. egg, hard boiled, sliced
Parsley

1½ T. French's
  horseradish mustard
¼ c. celery, chopped fine
½ t. season-all
¼ t. celery salt
1 pkg. crab/shrimp boil
Romaine lettuce to line dish
1 pt. cherry tomatoes

Boil shrimp in crab boil. Cool. Drain and peel. Line serving dish with Romaine lettuce leaves. Combine all remaining ingredients, except sliced boiled eggs. Pile on top of lettuce and garnish with boiled eggs, parsley, and cherry tomatoes.

Yield: about 5 cups

Sharron Brown Mayers
Baton Rouge, La.

HAWAIIAN SALAD

1 lb. can chunked pineapple,
  drained
1 lb. boiled ham, cubed
2 lg. Delicious apples, chunked

10-oz. block Longhorn
  cheese, cubed
10-oz. jar cherries,
  drained

Combine ingredients. Top with Sweet 'N Tart Glaze, Pina Colada flavor variation, page 21; or Poppy Seed Dressing, page 24. Cover and refrigerate at least one hour. Serve with fancy picks.

Yield: about 2 quarts

Becky Karavatakis
Lafayette, La.

COPPER PENNIES

2 lbs. carrots, sliced
1 green pepper, chopped
1 med. onion, chopped
½ c. celery, chopped
10.5-oz. can, undiluted,
   tomato soup

½ c. salad oil
¾ c. sugar
¾ c. vinegar
1 t. Worcestershire sauce
Salt and pepper, to taste
1 t. mustard

Boil carrots until tender-crisp. Drain and layer in bowl with green pepper, onion and celery. Mix tomato soup, salad oil, sugar, vinegar, Worcestershire, and mustard. Add salt and pepper, to taste. Pour over carrot mixture, cover and refrigerate several hours. Serve cold with picks or cocktail forks.

Yield: about 2½ pints

Irma Roesler Beisel
Leawood, Kansas

CARROT DAISIES

5 short, wide carrots
   about 1 lb.
1 c. rice vinegar

¼ c. honey
½ c. orange juice
1 T. pickle spices

Peel carrots. Slice about ¼″ thick. Combine vinegar, honey, orange juice and spices. Add carrots. Bring to boil. Reduce to medium-low heat. Cook 8 to 10 minutes, until tender-crisp. Drain; reserve syrup. Cool on wire rack. Use aspic cutter and cut into daisy (or your favorite) shape. Place carrots in glass dish; cover with syrup. Cover dish and refrigerate overnight. Drain and serve.

Yield: 7 to 8 dozen

Becky Karavatakis
Lafayette, La.

LIGHT VEGETABLE PLATTER

1 c. cauliflower	1 c. broccoli
1 c. snow peas	1 c. thin carrot sticks
1 c. mushroom caps	1 c. thin celery sticks

Place a small custard cup upside down in center of 12" pyrex platter. Arrange vegetables around cup. Cover with plastic wrap. Make small incision in center to allow steam to escape. Place in microwave on high for 6 minutes, turning each 1½ minutes. Let rest 3 to 5 minutes after removing from oven. Be careful when removing plastic wrap as this will be very hot.

Yield: 6 cups

LIGHT ARTICHOKES IN FRENCH DRESSING

14-oz. can artichoke hearts	Optional: salt
4 T. lemon juice	1 T. ketchup
2 T. powdered pectin	¼ t. paprika
½ c. water	

Reserve salt. Combine remaining ingredients and shake well. Add salt, if desired. Rinse and drain artichokes; cut into quarters. Place in Zip-lock bag. Pour dressing over artichokes, press out air, seal and refrigerate overnight.

Yield: 28 to 32 pieces

Becky Karavatakis
Lafayette, La.

FRUIT COMPOTE

Apples
Banana
Nectarine
Watermelon
Honey Dew Melon
Cantaloupe

Strawberries
Raspberries
Seedless red and white grapes
Pineapple
Juice of 1 lemon

Peel, core, and chunk or slice fruit. Wash and hull berries. Wash and stem grapes. Reserve pineapple juice and mix with lemon juice and pour over fruit to prevent browning. Cover and refrigrate. Serve from carved out watermelon or from serving dish plain with picks. Serve with Poppy Seed Dressing, (page 24) or Avocado/Poppy Seed Dressing, (page 25) or marinate fruit in either dressing.

Variation: For Vegetable Compote: use celery sticks, carrot sticks, zucchini rounds, and cauliflower flowerettes. Boil for 1 minute; drain and marinate with choice of dressings; refrigerate at least 1 hour.

Yield: As much as you need

Becky Karavatakis
Lafayette, La.

CRACKERS/BREADS

SOUFFLE CRACKERS

Melted butter
Ice water
Saltine crackers

Preheat oven to 400° F. Brush baking sheet with melted butter. Fill large bowl with ice water. Add crackers and allow to absorb water for about 30 seconds. Using a slotted spatula remove crackers, drain and transfer to baking sheet. Carefully brush or drizzle melted butter, covering completely (be careful not to flatten crackers). Bake 15 minutes. Reduce oven heat to 300° F. and continue baking until golden brown, about 20 to 25 minutes. Cool on wire rack. Store in airtight container.

Yield: as many as you need

Vivian Mays
Lafayette, La.

THE WHITE HOUSE
WASHINGTON

December 16, 1985

Dear Mr. and Mrs. Karavatakis:

On behalf of Mrs. Reagan, thank you for taking the time to write to her. She wanted me to acknowledge your letter.

The "Souffle Cracker" is served in the White House Mess, however, they have served it for many years, an old navy recipe, they say. You are welcome to use the recipe and say it is served in the White House, but Mrs. Reagan didn't introduce it.

With the First Lady's best wishes,

Sincerely,

Deborah Balfour
Deputy Director of Projects
Office of the First Lady

OYSTER CRACKERS LOU

16-oz. pkg. Nabisco
   Oyster Crackers
⅔ c. vegetable oil

1 pkg. Original Ranch
   Dressing Mix
2 T. dry dill weed

Place crackers in large pan. Mix oil, dressing mix, and dill weed in bowl. Pour over crackers and stir well. Stir every 15 to 20 minutes until all liquid is absorbed. Store in airtight containers.

Yield: about 8 cups

Lou Ingram
Evergreen, Colorado

ITALIAN BREAD STICKS

2 sticks margarine
½ c. red wine vinegar
2 T. water
1 pkg. hamburger buns

1 pkg. Good Seasons
   salad dressing mix
⅓ c. salad oil

Melt margarine; allow to cool. Mix red wine vinegar, water and salad dressing mix; stir or shake well. Add salad oil; stir or shake well. Mix salad dressing with melted margarine. Slice hamburger buns into ½" strips. Roll or dip bread strips in mixture. Shake off excess. Place on baking sheet. Preheat oven to 450° F. Place baking sheet in oven, wait 1 minute, then turn oven to 200° F. Do not open the oven door. After 2 hours turn the bread sticks over. Continue at 200° F. for 2 more hours.

Yield: about 5 dozen

Kay Dillard
LaPlace, La.

WHEAT STICKS

1 pkg. dry yeast
1 t. honey
1½ c. water (105-115° F.)
2 c. whole wheat flour

1 to 1¼ c. flour
1 t. salt
2 T. olive oil
Olive oil

Dissolve yeast and honey in warm water. Let stand until bubbly. Mix whole wheat flour, 1 cup of all purpose flour, and salt in large bowl. Make a well in center and pour in half yeast and mix well. Stir in 2 tablespoons olive oil and remaining yeast mixture to form a sticky dough. Turn out on well-floured board and knead in additional flour to form a soft dough. Knead until smooth and elastic, about 10 minutes. Place in a well greased bowl, cover and let rise in warm place for about 45 minutes or until doubled. Punch down and knead again 2 to 3 minutes. Let rise again until doubled, about 30 minutes. Heat oven to 450° F. Grease baking sheet with olive oil. Punch down dough and divide dough into 24 equal pieces. Roll each piece to about 12 x 1 inch wide. Cut into 3" pieces. Place about 1" apart and brush lightly with olive oil. Bake until crisp and light golden, about 18 to 20 minutes. Cool on wire racks. Store in airtight containers. Freezes well for up to 6 months. Return to slow oven, about 225° F. to recrisp before serving.

Yield: 8 dozen

Becky Karavatakis
Lafayette, La.

ONION STICKS

1 env. onion soup mix

1 lb. sharp cheddar
  cheese, grated

1 lb. butter

¼ c. dry white wine

2 c. flour

½ t. salt

Optional: sesame seeds

Process to form a ball. Divide into tablespoonful balls. Roll each to 4'' stick. Place on lightly greased baking sheet and bake at 400° F. for 10 to 12 minutes or golden. If desired, roll in sesame seeds.

Yield: 7 to 8 dozen

Sharron Mayers
Baton Rouge, La.

BENNE SEED WAFERS

2 c. flour

1 t. salt

1 c. roasted benne seeds *
  (sesame seeds)

¾ c. butter

¼ c. ice water

⅛ t. cayenne pepper

Mix flour, salt, and cayenne pepper. Cut in butter. Add enough water to make the consistency of pie crust. Add benne seeds. Roll between ¼'' and ⅛'' and cut with biscuit cutter. Place on cookie sheet and bake at 325° F. for 20 to 25 minutes or until lightly golden in color. Sprinkle with salt as soon as removed from oven. Transfer to rack for cooling. May be kept in covered tin or jar. Before using, place in a slow oven (about 225° F.) to crisp.

Yield: 3 to 4 dozen

Trudy Williams
Houston, Texas

CHEESE CRISPIES

½ lb. sharp cheddar cheese
3 T. butter, softened
¾ c. flour
½ t. celery powder
2 t. Worcestershire sauce

½ t. salt
¼ t. white pepper
Grated Parmesan cheese
Paprika

Grate cheese. Add butter and blend. Add flour, celery powder, Worcestershire, salt and pepper. Mix well to form stiff dough. Divide in half and form 2 rolls about 1¼" in diameter. Wrap in plastic wrap; chill until firm. Preheat oven to 450° F. Slice rolls into ¼" wafers and arrange on lightly greased cookie sheets. Sprinkle with Parmesan cheese and paprika. Bake 8 to 10 minutes or until puffed and golden brown. Cool on wire rack. Serve at room temperature.

Yield: 4 to 5 dozen

Celia Pope
Baton Rouge, La.

REFRIGERATOR CHEESE WAFERS

½ lb. sharp cheddar, grated
1½ c. flour
1½ t. salt

1 stick butter, creamed
Optional: ¼ c. fine chopped
pecans or almonds

Process to form a ball. Divide into two rolls. Roll each one into tube shape. Roll in nuts if desired. Wrap in wax paper and chill 1 to 2 hours. Slice about ⅛" thick and bake at 350° F. for 8 to 10 minutes or until golden. Remove to wire rack to cool. May be frozen up to 4 months.

Yield: 6 to 8 dozen

Becky Karavatakis
Lafayette, La.

DANISH BLEU WAFERS

¼ c. butter
3 oz. Bleu cheese
  crumbled

1 c. unbleached flour
4 t. milk
Sesame seeds

Reserve sesame seeds. Process remaining ingredients to form a ball. Refrigerate 1 hour. Roll out ⅛" thick and cut into rectangle or square shapes. Sprinkle tops with sesame seeds. Bake on ungreased cookie sheets in preheated 400° F. oven for 5 to 6 minutes, or lightly golden. Cool completely on wire rack. Store in air tight container.

Variation: for a milder cracker, use cream cheese.

Yield: 30 to 48

Becky Karavatakis
Lafayette, La.

CHEESE THINS

1 c. flour
1 c. Rice Krispies cereal
1 c. packed, grated cheddar cheese
6 doz. smoked almonds

1 stick butter
¼ t. Tony's seasoning
¼ t. Beau Monde seasoning
6 doz. pecan halves

Mix together, except nuts, and roll into ¾" balls. Place on cookie sheet and press with fork. Press nut into center. Bake at 350° F. until light golden. Cool on rack and store in airtight container.

Yield: about 12 dozen

Sharron Brown Mayers
Baton Rouge, La.

BAGELS

1 env. dry yeast	1 lg. egg, separated
¼ c. warm water (110° F.)	4 c. flour
¼ c. butter	2 qts. water
1 T. sugar	2 T. sugar
1 t. salt	1 T. water
1 c. water	Optional: poppy or sesame seeds

Stir yeast into ¼ c. warm water until dissolved. Add butter, 1 table-spoon sugar, salt, 1 cup water, egg white and 1½ cups flour. Beat with electric mixer about 3 minutes until smooth. Add enough of the remaining flour to make a soft dough. Turn out on floured board and knead about 5 minutes or until smooth and elastic. Place dough in greased bowl and turn to grease all sides. Cover and reserve to warm place to double in bulk, about 1 hour. Punch down; knead 1 to 2 minutes. Divide into 4 pieces; divide each into 10 pieces. Roll each piece to 6" rope and form a circle, pinching ends together to seal. Let rest for 15 minutes. Heat 2 quarts water and 2 tablespoons sugar to a simmer, DO NOT BOIL. Grease 2 baking sheets, reserve. Use sloted spoon and lower 3 to 4 bagels into water at a time; cook 1 minute on each side. Remove and drain on paper towels. Arrange on buttered baking sheet. Preheat oven to 400° F. Beat egg yolk with 1 tablespoon water. Brush bagel tops with egg mixture. Sprinkle with poppy or sesame seeds, if desired. Bake about 15 minutes or until lightly browned.

Yield: 40 2" bagels

Becky Karavatakis
Lafayette, La.

SOFT PRETZELS

3¾ c. flour
1 env. dry yeast
1¼ c. milk
½ c. butter
1 T. sugar

½ t. salt
1 lg. egg, separated
1 T. water
Coarse salt or sesame seeds

Combine 1½ cups flour and yeast. Make a well in center; reserve. Combine milk, butter, sugar and salt in sauce pan. Stir over low heat until butter is melted. Cool slightly. Pour warm milk mixture and unbeaten egg white into well in flour. Beat 3 minutes with electric mixer. Stir in enough remaining flour to make a soft dough. Turn out on floured board and knead about 5 minutes until smooth and elastic. Place in greased bowl and turn to grease all sides. Cover and reserve to double in bulk, about 1 hour. Punch down; let rest 10 minutes. Divide into 6 pieces. Divide again in half. Divide each piece into 5 pieces. Roll each piece to 8″ rope. Shape and pinch ends together. Let rest for 15 minutes. Pour 4″ water in 4 quart pot; bring to simmer over medium heat, Do Not Boil. Grease 3 baking sheets. Using slotted spoon, lower 3 to 4 pretzels into water; cook 30 seconds on each side. Remove and drain on paper towels. Arrange on baking sheets. Beat egg yolk with 1 tablespoon water. Brush tops of pretzels. Sprinkle with coarse salt or sesame seeds. Bake in preheated oven at 400° F. for 10 to 12 minutes until lightly browned.

Yield: 50

Becky Karavatakis
Lafayette, La.

ONION HORN ROLLS

1 pkg. dry yeast	1 lg. egg, beaten
¼ c. warm water, (105° F.)	6 to 7 c. flour
2 c. milk, scalded	8 oz. Cheddar, shredded
¼ c. butter	2 T. dry minced onion
1 t. salt	1 T. butter, melted

Dissolve yeast in water, reserve. Combine hot milk, ¼ c. butter, sugar, and salt until butter is melted; cool slightly. Add egg, yeast mixture and 2 cups of flour. Mix well. Stir in cheese, onion and enough flour to make a soft dough. Knead on floured board 8 to 10 minutes or until smooth. Form into ball, place in well-greased bowl and rub melted butter over top. Cover; let rise at 85° F. for about 1½ hours (double bulk). Punch down; divide into 4 equal parts. Roll each part to 11 to 12 inch circle. Cut each circle into 16 wedges. Roll up from large end to small end. Place on greased baking sheets about 2 inches apart. Cover with smooth towel and let rise at 85° F. for 1½ hours (double bulk). Bake in preheated oven at 375° F. for 8 to 10 minutes or until golden brown.

Yield: 64 horns

Becky Karavatakis
Lafayette, La.

IRMA'S SWEDISH BUTTER HORNS

4 c. flour
¼ c. sugar
1 c. milk
1 cake yeast, dissolved in
  ¼ c. water

1 c. margarine
½ t. salt
2 lg. eggs

Beat eggs and milk. Mix together with yeast and ¾ cup melted margarine. Mix in dry ingredients. Refrigerate overnight. Divide into 12 equal parts. Roll each part into a circle bout 6" across. Brush melted margarine over each circle. Divide into 8 pie-shaped parts. Roll up from large end to small end, and pinch ends to seal. Brush remaining melted margarine on top and let rise until double in size (about 1 hour). Bake in 375° F. oven for 8 to 10 minutes, or until golden.

Yield: about 6 dozen

Irma Roesler Beisel
Leawood, Kansas

MINI DINNER ROLLS

2 pkg. yeast
2 c. warm water, (105° F.)
4 c. self-rising flour

½ c. sugar
¾ c. oil
1 lg. egg

Mix yeast with warm water until yeast is dissolved. Add sugar, oil and egg. Blend together. Add flour and mix together. Refrigerate in covered container until ready to use. Grease mini muffin tins and fill ¾ full and bake at 400° F. for 8 to 10 minutes or until tops golden.

Yield: about 3 dozen

Carol Christie
Lafayette, La.

MINI BURGER BUNS

½ c. milk
2 sticks butter
2 pkgs. dry yeast
½ c. warm water (110° F.)
½ c. sugar
1 t. salt

3 c. unbleached flour
1 c. whole wheat flour
3 lg. eggs, beaten
1 t. lemon peeled, grated
Optional: toasted sesame seeds
or poppy seeds

Scald milk; add butter, stirring until melted. Dissolve yeast in warm water. Pour milk mixture over sugar and salt. Stir to dissolve. Add yeast mixture, eggs, and lemon peel. Sift flours together; stir in 1 cup at a time. Cover and let rise in refrigerator overnight. Punch down and roll into 48 balls. Flatten each slightly to 1½″ diameter and place on greased baking sheet. Sprinkle with sesame or poppy seeds if desired. Cover with towel and let rise until double in bulk, about 1½ to 2 hours. Bake at 350° F. for 12 to 15 minutes until golden. Cool on wire racks. May be frozen at this point in airtight freezer containers.

Yield: 4 dozen

ROQUEFORT BISQUITS

4-oz. Roquefort cheese
1 stick butter
1⅓ c. flour

2 T. whipping cream
1 lg. egg yolk
1 lg. egg white

Process to form ball. Chill. Roll to ¼″ thick. Cut into 1¼″ to 1½″ rounds. Beat egg white with 1 tablespoon water. Brush tops with egg mixture. Bake at 425° F. for 10 to 12 minutes or until golden.

Yield: 3 to 4 dozen

Becky Karavatakis
Lafayette, La.

FRENCH BREAD FINGER BUNS

1 pkg. dry yeast
2 c. warm water (100° F.)
5 c. flour
2-3 T. cornmeal

1 T. salt
2 t. sugar
3 T. melted butter

Dissolve yeast in water, sugar and salt. Combine flour and yeast mixture. Process to form a ball. Knead on floured board 3 to 4 minutes. Put in greased bowl, turn and cover with slightly damp cloth. Let rise at 85° F. until double in bulk (about 1½ hours). Grease 2 large baking sheets; dust each with cornmeal. Divide dough into thirds and roll to 8" x 15" rectangle. Cut each into 4" x 3" rectangle. Roll each from long side; pinch at seam. Place seam down on baking sheet. Brush tops lightly with butter. Make 2 diagonal slits in the top of each, about ¼" deep. Cover; let rise 35 to 40 minutes. Bake at 450° F. for 5 minutes; reduce heat to 350° F. and continue baking 6 to 8 minutes longer or until tops are golden brown. Remove to racks for cooling.

Yield: 30

Becky Karavatakis
Lafayette, La.

ETHEL'S HUSH PUPPIES

1 c. flour
1 c. yellow corn meal
½ c. sugar
1 t. salt

1 t. baking powder
1 lg. egg
½ c. milk
Dash red or black pepper

Mix flour, meal, and sugar. Add salt, baking powder and pepper. Add egg and milk. Mix until stiff. Drop by teaspoonsful into hot deep oil (375° F.). Remove when golden. Drain on paper towels.

Yield: about 3 dozen

Ethel Thomas
Baton Rouge, La.

POLENTA ACADIANA

3 pts. water
2 c. yellow cornmeal
6 slices bacon, fried
   crisp, crumbled
6 green onion tops,
   sliced thin

2 t. Tony's seasoning
¼ c. peanut oil
2 Jalapeno peppers,
   minced
Anchovy Salsa

Bring water, bacon, onions, and Tony's seasoning to rapid boil in large pot. Whisk vigorously and add cornmeal slowly, but steadily. Reduce heat to low, stir often and cook until very thick, 45 minutes to one hour. (Wooden spoon will stand upright, unsupported.) Grease a 9″ x 12″ x 2″ cake pan. Press mixture into pan and pound several times to release air bubbles. Let stand at room temperature, un-covered, for at least 4 to 6 hour. Turn out onto cutting board and cut into pieces about 1″ x 2″ in length. Heat oil in iron skillet over medium heat. Carefully fry polenta, until golden on all sides. Serve warm with Anchovy Salsa.

Anchovy Salsa
1 pt. whipping cream
2 sm. cloves garlic, minced

8 anchovy fillets
drained, minced

Heat cream to boiling; reduce heat to medium low. Cook, stirring often, until cream is reduced in half. (About 20 minutes.) Melt butter over low heat; add garlic and anchovies. Cook; mashing anchovies and garlic against edge of pot until well blended and almost smooth. Stir in cream until sauce is smooth and hot, DO NOT BOIL. Serve warm. DOES NOT KEEP — use within 2 hours. Makes 1 cup.

Yield: about 54

Becky Karavatakis
Lafayette, La.

LITTLE POCKETS

1 env. dry yeast
1 t. sugar
¼ c. warm water
  (110° F.)
4 c. flour

1 t. salt
2 T. olive oil
1½ c. warm water
  (110° F.)

Dissolve yeast and sugar in ¼ c. warm water; rest 5 minutes until foamy. Combine flour and salt. Make a well in center; add yeast mixture, oil and 1½ cups warm water. Slowly add flour in; mix well. Knead on floured board 7 to 8 minutes or until smooth, adding more flour if necessary to make stiff dough. Place in greased bowl and turn to grease all sides. Cover and reserve to warm place to double in bulk, about 1¼ hours. Grease 3 baking sheets. Punch down dough; knead 1 to 2 minutes. Divide into 6 pieces. Divide again into 6 pieces. Roll each piece to 3" circles. Arrange 12 to pan. Cover and let rise in warm place until doubled, about 40 minutes. Preheat oven to 500° F. Place rack in center of oven; bake 1 pan at a time, about 5 minutes until puffed and lightly browned. Let cool. May be frozen at this point in airtight freezer container. Cut in half.

Yield: 72

Becky Karavatakis
Lafayette, La.

PASTRIES/FILLINGS

RAMEKINS OF SHRIMP
IN SOUR CREAM

1½ lbs. raw shrimp, headless
⅓ c. butter
½ lb. mushrooms, thinly sliced
1½ c. sour cream
Salt and pepper to taste

2 t. soy sauce
Dash paprika
⅓ c. buttered bread
Crumbs

Shell and devein shrimp. Wash and dry well. Saute in hot butter for 2 minutes with mushrooms. Heat sour cream to boiling point and season well with salt, pepper, soy and just enough paprika to give a rich pink tint. Combine thoroughly the seasoned cream and shrimp mixtures and cook over low heat until sauce is thick and smooth. Divide mixture into 6 buttered individual ramekins and sprinkle with buttered bread crumbs. Brown ramekins under broiler just before serving. May be served in prebaked Mini Tart Shells (p. 59).

Yield: 6 dinner size or
    3 to 4 dozen mini size

Eva Dell Daigre
Lafayette, La.

BROCCOLI AND SHRIMP CASSEROLE

3 lb. bag frozen chopped
  broccoli
6½ oz. can sm. shrimp
1 c. chinese noodles
¼ c. butter

6½ oz. can sliced water
chestnuts
10½ oz. can Campbell's cream
of spinach soup, undiluted
½ t. Tony's seasoning

Reserve noodles. Cook broccoli; drain. Combine with other ingredients and mix well. Pour into casserole dish; top with noodles and bake at 350° F. for 15 to 20 minutes. Serve warm with shells for filling.

Yield: about 3½ pints

Sharron Brown Mayers
Baton Rouge, La.

CURRIED CRAB

1 c. mayonnaise
1 lg. egg yolk
2 t. curry powder
6 green onions w/tops,
  minced bottom; thin
  sliced tops

2 c. lump crab meat
½ c. cucumber, peeled,
  seeded and chopped
1 T. gingerroot, minced
Salt and white pepper
48 Mini Tart Shells (p. 59)

Blend together mayonnaise, egg yolk and curry powder. Combine crab, onions, cucumbers, and gingerroot. Gently fold into mayonnaise mixture. Add salt and white pepper to taste. Fill tart shells; place under hot broiler until golden, watching closely not to burn.

Variation: Replace the crab with cooked chicken breast.

Yield: 48 mini tarts

DEVILED CRAB TARTS

½ c. Half and Half
2 T. butter
8 oz. white crab, flaked
½ c. cracker crumbs
Dash Tabasco

½ t. dry mustard
1 T. onion, minced
½ t. salt
½ t. horseradish
30 Mini Tart Shells (p. 59)

Heat butter in milk until melted. Stir in cracker crumbs. Remove from heat and add remaining ingredients. Blend well. Fill each tart shell with a well rounded teaspoon of mixture. Bake in 350° F. oven for 10 to 12 minutes. Garnish with parsley or slice of pimento stuffed olive.

Yield: about 30

Becky Karavatakis
Lafayette, La.

LOBSTER TARTS

1 6¾-oz. can lobster
¼ c. Parmesan, grated
1 c. cheddar, grated
¼ c. Italian dressing
30 Mini Tart Shells (p. 59)

1 lg. egg
¼ c. onions, minced
¼ c. Italian bread crumbs
¼ c. heavy cream
Salt and pepper, to taste

Mince lobster; combine with Parmesan, cheddar, dressing, egg and onion. Place a rounded teaspoonful into each tart shell. Cover each with ¼ t. heavy cream and sprinkle tops with bread crumbs. Bake at 350° F. 12 to 15 minutes. Serve warm.

Variation: omit lobster and use 2 tins smoked oysters, drained and minced. Add 1 pkg. frozen chopped spinach, cooked dry; add Tabasco to taste.

Yield: about 30

Becky Karavatakis
Lafayette, La.

MINI CHICKEN POT PIES

4 c. finely chopped
  cooked chicken
1 lb. frozen mixed peas
  and carrots

½ pt. breakfast cream
1 c. chicken broth
60 Mini Tart Shells (p. 59)
Salt and white pepper

Combine chicken, peas and carrots, and chicken broth. Season to taste with salt and pepper. Spoon into shells. Top with ½ teaspoon cream. Bake at 350° F. until tart is golden brown.

Yield: about 60

Becky Karavatakis
Lafayette, La.

POLYNESIAN HAM TARTS

2 T. butter
¼ t. curry powder
2 T. minced celery
2 T. scallions, minced
30 Mini Tart Shells, (p.59)
15 cherries, halved

1 c. boiled ham, minced
⅛ t. powdered mustard
3 T. mayonnaise
8½-oz. can pineapple,
crushed and drained

Prebake shells at 350° F. for 8 to 10 minutes until light golden. Saute onion, celery and ham in butter and curry powder until soft. Cool 10 to 15 minutes. Reserve cherries. Stir in remaining ingredients. Cover and refrigerate until ready to use. Spoon into shells and heat through. Garnish with cherry half, if desired. Serve warm.

Yield: about 30

MINI-TART SHELLS

1¼ c. flour
6 T. cold butter
   cut into bits

2 T. Crisco
¼ t. salt
3 T. cold water

Place flour and salt in processor. Process 15 seconds. Add remaining ingredients and process to form a ball. Wrap in plastic wrap and refrigerate at least one hour. Roll out to ⅛" thick on floured board. Cut out with flutted or daisy shaped 2½" cutter and fit into mini tart pans. Prick bottom with fork. May be frozen at this point for fillings that need to be baked. Bake at 350° F. for 12 to 15 minutes. May be frozen at this point for fillings that do not need to be baked.

Yield: about 4 dozen

Becky Karavatakis
Lafayette, La.

CRAB TARTS CAVIAR

8 lg. eggs, boiled and chopped
1 c. white crabmeat, flaked
⅓ c. green onions, with tops,
* fine chopped*
Salt and pepper to taste

¼ c. butter
2 c. sour cream
48 Cream Cheese Pastry Shells, baked
Caviar sauce

Melt butter; reserve to cool. Combine eggs, crabmeat and ¼ c. onions. Cream 1 cup sour cream with cooled butter. Add egg mixture; season to taste. Spoon into shells. Mix remaining onions with other cup of sour cream. Spread over crab mixture and top with Caviar Sauce.

Caviar Sauce:
1 c. mayonnaise
2 oz. jar black caviar
1½ T. lemon juice

1 t. chives, minced
1 t. dried parsley

Mix together mayonnaise, lemon juice, chives and parsley. Gently fold in caviar. Keep refrigerated until ready to use. Makes about 1¼ cups.

Yield: 48

CREAM CHEESE PASTRY SHELLS

3 oz. Philadelphia cream cheese
1 stick butter
1 c. flour

Process to form a ball. Chill for one hour. Roll pastry on floured board to ⅛″ thick. Cut with 2½″ round cutter. Press lightly into mini tart pans; prick bottoms with fork. May be frozen for fillings which need to be baked. Or bake at 350° F. for 12 to 15 minutes. May be frozen baked for fillings needing pre-baked shells.

Yield: about 30

Becky Karavatakis
Lafayette, La.

OVEN FRIED PIES

2 recipes Turnover pastry (p.63)
Filling
Mustard Piquant Sauce

Roll pastry out on lightly floured board. Roll to ⅛'' thick and cut with 2½'' cutter. Place ½ to ¾ teaspoon filling in center and fold over. Seal with a fork. Place on greased cookie sheet and bake at 375° F. 8 to 10 minutes, or until golden. Serve warm with Mustard Piquant Sauce for dipping.

Filling:

1 lb. ground round	*8 oz. sour cream*
1 lg. onion, chopped fine	*Dash of cinnamon*
2 T. tomato paste	*Dash nutmeg*
Juice of one lemon	*Salt & pepper, to taste*

Brown meat and onion. Add remaining ingredients and simmer 5 minutes. Refrigerate.

Mustard Piquant Sauce:

1 c. cider vinegar	*3 lg. eggs*
¾ c. dry mustard	*1 c. honey*
1 T. horseradish	*¼ t. Tabasco or to taste*

Process. Cook over double boiler until thick as table mustard, stirring occasionally. Refrigerate. Makes 2½ cups.

Yield: about 100

Becky Karavatakis
Lafayette, La.

PASTRY TURNOVERS

1 batch Turnover Pastry (p. 63)   *Choice of Fillings*

Chicken Filling
7 chicken legs   *½ t. salt*
½ t. black pepper   *¼ t. Tony's seasoning*
¼ t. lemon pepper   *¼ c. celery, chopped fine*
1 can Campbell's cream of   *1 qt. water*
   mushroom soup, UNDILUTED

Boil chicken in water with peppers, salts, and celery. Remove chicken from bone and chop fine. Mix chicken with undiluted soup. Makes about 5 dozen.

Squeeze 'N Go Fruit Filling
Kraft squeeze Orange Marmalade   *1 lg. egg, beaten*
Kraft squeeze Strawberry Preserves   *cinnamon sugar*

Squeeze onto center of pastry, fold over, seal with fork. Brush tops with beaten egg, sprinkle with cinnamon sugar if desired. Makes about 5 dozen.

Meat Filling
3¼ lb. ground round   *¼ c. melted margarine*
1 lg. onion, finely grated   *¼ t. season-all salt*
¼ t. Tony's seasoning   *½ t. black pepper*

Saute onions in margarine. Add seasonings. Add meat to onions and brown. Place 1 level teaspoonful mixture in center and fold over. Seal edges with fork. Sprinkle top with paprika. Makes about 10 dozen.

Sharron Brown Mayers
Baton Rouge, La.

HAM TURNOVERS

¾ c. ground ham
2 T. hot ketchup
1½ t. Creole mustard

½ t. Worcestershire sauce
1-2 dashes Tabasco
1 batch Turnover Pastry

Combine ham, ketchup, mustard, Worcestershire and Tabasco. Place scant teaspoon of filling in center and fold. Prick edges with fork. Place on ungreased baking sheet and bake at 400° F. for 10 to 12 minutes or until golden brown.

Yield: about 30

Becky Karavatakis
Lafayette, La.

TURNOVER PASTRY

2 c. flour
¼ t. salt
1 c. soft butter

8-oz. cream cheese, softened
1 lg. egg, beaten

Sift flour and salt. Cut in butter and cream cheese with pastry blender or two knives. Roll into ball and chill at least one hour. Roll out very thin on floured board and cut into 2½" circles. Place 1 level teaspoonful filling in center and fold over. Press edges together with fork. Brush tops with beaten egg. Bake at 400° F. about 20 minutes or until golden brown.

Yield: about 5 dozen

Sharron Brown Mayers
Baton Rouge, La.

LA PETITE PUFFS

La Petite Puff Shells (p.65)   *Choice of fillings*

Shrimp, Lobster, Crawfish or Crab

1 c. boiled, chopped, shrimp   *8 oz. soft cream cheese*
lobster, crawfish or lump crab   *1 t. Worcestershire*
¼ c. fine chopped onions   *1 t. Tony's Seasoning*
2 t. lemon juice   *1-2 dashes Tabasco*
½ t. horseradish

Combine. Chill at least 1 hour. Keep refrigerated until ready to use. May be served hot or cold. Fill just prior to serving.

Chicken, Ham or Tuna

2 c. fine chopped chicken   *⅓ c. mayonnaise*
   or 2 c. fine chopped ham   *2 t. Creole mustard*
   or 2 6½-oz. cans tuna   *½ t. lemon juice*
1 t. fine chopped onion   *½ t. Italian seasoning*
½ t. Tony's Seasoning   *3 T. chopped celery*
  (¼ t. for ham or tuna)   *1 T. chopped parsley*

Combine. Serve as above.

Variation: omit mayonnaise and mustard. Add 1 can condensed cream of mushroom or cream of cheddar cheese soup, undiluted. Heat this version and serve from chafing dish with puffs for filling.

Yield: 4 to 5 dozen   *Becky Karavatakis*
     Lafayette, La.

CREAM de CRAB

2 8-oz. cream cheese, softened
1 c. Hellmann's mayonnaise
2 T. lemon juice
1 t. Worcestershire sauce
2 t. flour
60 La Petite Puff Shells

1 lb. white crabmeat,
picked and flaked
⅔ c. almonds, slivered
and toasted
Dash cayenne pepper
Salt to taste

Process cheese with mayonnaise, lemon juice, Worcestershire sauce, flour and pepper. Gently stir in crabmeat and almonds; add salt to taste. Bake in covered casserole dish at 300° F. for 20 minutes. Serve warm from chafing dish with La Petite Puff Shells or melba rounds.

Yield: about 5 cups

LA PETITE PUFF SHELLS

½ c. butter
1 c. flour
4 lg. eggs

1 c. water
1 t. salt

Combine butter, salt and water. Bring to boil; reduce to low heat and add flour. Beat until a ball forms. Remove from heat and beat in one egg at a time. Beat until shiny. Drop by rounded teaspoonsful onto baking sheet. Bake at 375° F. for 10 minutes or until golden in color.

Yield: about 4 dozen

Becky Karavatakis
Lafayette, La.

RUSSIAN PIROGS WITH YOGURT SAUCE

2 lg. yellow onions,
  chopped fine
1 T. unsalted butter
¼ c. Cognac
3 lg. eggs
2½ t. salt
1½ t. dry mustard
¾ t. ground allspice
1 lg. egg, lightly beaten
  with 1 T. water

½ t. white pepper
¼ t. ground cloves
2 lbs. lean ground pork
1 lb. ground round
6-oz. shredded Jarlsberg
  cheese
¼ c. sunflower seeds,
  roasted and shelled
¾ t. coriander
1 batch Pirog Dough (p. 67)

Make Pirog Dough. Prepare Yogurt Sauce. Saute onions in butter until soft. Remove from heat and stir in Cognac. Let cool. Beat eggs, beat in salt, mustard, allspice, coriander, pepper and cloves. Stir in onion mixture, pork, beef, cheese and sunflower seeds. Divide dough. Roll out to about 16″ circles. Cut into 2½″ rounds. Place 1 tablespoonful of filling near center and fold over, pressing out air bubbles. Press seam with fork tines to seal. Reroll scraps and cut into small leaf shapes. Attach 3 leaves to each pirog with egg white. Brush entire top with egg white. Bake at 350° F. for 12 to 15 minutes or until golden brown. Cool on wire racks. Serve at room temperature with Yogurt Sauce.

Yogurt Sauce
1 c. plain yogurt
1 c. sour cream

Dash Tabasco
1 T. chives, chopped fine

Combine yogurt, sour cream and Tabasco. Refrigerate at least one hour. Garnish with chives. Makes 2 cups.

Yield: about 3 dozen

Becky Karavatakis
Lafayette, La.

PIROG DOUGH

1 pkg. dry yeast
½ c. water (110°F.)
2¼ c. flour
1 t. sugar

¼ t. salt
3 large eggs
1¼ sticks butter,
softened, unsalted

Dissolve yeast in water and let stand 10 minutes. Beat in ½ cup flour, the sugar and salt. Beat in eggs, one at a time until smooth. Beat in butter, 2 tablespoonsful at a time until smooth. Add remaining flour a little at a time. Beat at medium-high for 5 minutes. Cover and let rise in warm place to double, about one hour. Punch down, cover, and refrigerate overnight.

Yield: 3 dozen

TORTILLAS

2 c. masa harina
1 to 1¼ c. warm water

Mix flour and 1 cup water together. Add a little water at a time until you have a soft dough. Divide dough into 2 equal parts. Divide each half into 16 equal parts. Roll each part into a ball and flatten in tortilla press. Heat one heavy skillet to 375° F. and a second to 350° F. Place one tortilla in hot skillet for 30 seconds. Turn tortilla into other skillet for about 1 minute. Turn and cook for additional 30 seconds. Keep warm between towels.

Yield: 30 to 32 2½″

Becky Karavatakis
Lafayette, La.

CHEESE BLINTZES

1 lb. dry cottage cheese
4 oz. Philadelphia cream
   cheese
2 lg. egg yolks
1 t. salt

1 T. sour cream
1 T. butter
1½ T. sugar
Dash of white pepper
1 batch Blintzes

Combine ingredients and blend well. Place a rounded teaspoon of mixture in center of the browned side; fold sides over like an envelop. Fry in buttered skillet over medium-high heat, until browned. Top with additional sour cream or powdered sugar, if desired.

Yield: about 2 dozen

BLINTZES

4 lg. eggs, beaten
1 c. flour

Dash of salt
1 c. water

Combine ingredients and beat until smooth. Heat small skillet to 375° F. Brush or spray lightly with oil. Pour scant 2 tablespoons butter into pan. When edges start curling, turn out onto platter. Grease pan as needed.

Yield: about 2 dozen

Leslie Henfield
Baton Rouge, La.

AVOCADO AND SHRIMP CREPES

2 T. butter
3 T. flour
1½ c. milk, warmed
2 oz. Swiss cheese, shredded
2 T. dry white wine
¼ c. butter, melted
1 avocado, sliced thin

2 T. teriyaki sauce
1 t. Worcestershire
½ t. salt
¼ t. pepper
1 lb. shrimp, peeled
deveined and minced
1 T. lemon juice
1 batch Crepes

Melt 2 tablespoons butter over medium heat; stir in flour. Cook about 3 minutes. Stir in warmed milk and continue stirring until mixture begins to thicken. Add cheese and stir until cheese melts and sauce thickens. Stir in wine, teriyaki, Worcestershire, salt and pepper. Fold shrimp into sauce. Sprinkle lemon juice over avocado and reserve. Place one scant tablespoon of filling on end of crepe and roll up. Place rolls in baking dish, brush with melted butter. Run under broiler until golden. Garnish with thin slice of avocado and serve warm.

CREPES

1¼ c. flour
4 lg. eggs
1 c. milk

3 T. unsalted butter,
melted
½ t. salt

Put ingredients in blender or processor and process about half a minute. Scrape down and process another half minute. Pour into glass pitcher; cover and refrigerate at least one hour. Pour scant tablespoonful batter onto grill at medium-high and cook until bubbles begin to burst. Turn and cook about half minute longer.

Yield: about 3 dozen

Becky Karavatakis
Lafayette, La.

SPRING ROLLS IN HAWAIIAN PLUM SAUCE

Spring Roll Wrappers
½ lb. lean pork
½ lb. chicken breast
1 clove garlic, minced
2 T. peanut oil
2 T. soy sauce

4 oz. bamboo shoots
1 T. gingerroot,
minced
2 T. oyster sauce
½ T. molasses
Peanut oil for frying

Prepare plum sauce. Make Spring Roll Wrappers (p. 71). Cut pork, chicken and bamboo shoots into 1 x ¼ x ¼ inch strips. Saute pork, chicken and garlic in 2 tablespoons oil until cooked. Add onions and bamboo shoots. Saute 3 minutes longer. Stir in ginger, soy, oyster sauce and molasses. Place scant 2 tablespoonful at one end of wrapper. Roll up to cover filling. Fold in sides and finish rolling. Moisten edges with water and press gently to seal. Pan fry in 1 inch of peanut oil at 375° F. Fry 3 to 4 at a time, turning once until golden brown. Drain on paper towels. Cut in half just before serving. Serve warm.

Note: 1 lb. won ton wraps can be used; fill with scant tablespoonful, fold over ends and roll up. Seal with water.

Plum Sauce
½ c. apple cider vinegar
½ c. plum jelly
¼ c. mango chutney,
finely chopped

¼ c. hoisin sauce
¼ c. packed brown sugar
¼ c. honey

Combine and heat until boiling. Reduce heat and simmer, stirring occasionally for 20 minutes. Cool. Transfer to pint jar and refrigerate. Makes about 1 pint.

Yield: 36 halves

Becky Karavatakis
Lafayette, La.

SPRING ROLL WRAPPERS

2 c. flour
2 c. water

Mix flour and water in medium-sized bowl until smooth. Heat small nonstick skillet (I use a 6''x 6'' square skillet) over low heat. Brush a thin layer of batter over bottom of skillet with pastry brush. As batter sets add an additional layer, making sure that all holes are filled. Cook just until edges begin to pull away from pan. Peel off and stack between layers of waxed paper.

Yield: about 18

Becky Karavatakis
Lafayette, La.

CRABMEAT CHEESE WON TONS

8 oz. Philadelphia cream,
* softened*
2 oz. grated cheddar cheese,
* softened*
4 oz. crab meat

Salt and pepper, to taste
1 lb. pkg. won ton wrappers
1 lg. egg, beaten w/1 t.
water

Mix cheeses. Mix in crab. Season to taste with salt and pepper. Place one teaspoonful mixture in center of wrapper. To make flower shape fold over at an angle so that the three triangles at the top are about equal in size. Curve right side around to center of bottom; brush edge with egg mixture. Curve left side around and seal at edge. Heat oil to 375° F. and fry until golden. Drain; serve warm. Note: Can be made by simply folding over to form triangle and sealing edges.

Yield: about 4 dozen

Linda Lee Mashburn
GOLDEN CHINA RESTAURANT
Lafayette, La.

PORK AND CRAB EGG ROLLS

4-oz. lean boneless pork
  loin, cut ⅛'' x ⅛'' x 1''
2 T. rice vinegar
3 t. cornstarch
2-oz. bamboo shoots, drained,
  cut ⅛'' x ⅛'' x 1''
½ sm. green bell pepper,
  cut ⅛'' x ⅛'' x 1''
2-oz. fresh white crab,
  picked and flaked
1 sm. egg, beaten

1 T. peanut oil
1 scallion, minced
1 t. fresh ginger root,
  pared, minced
1 c. celery cabbage,
  fine shredded
1 t. sesame oil
½ lb. won ton wraps
3 med. dried black mushrooms
4 c. peanut oil for frying

Combine pork, 1 tablespoon vinegar and 2 teaspoons cornstarch. Marinate 30 minutes. Mix 1 t. cornstarch and 1 tablespoon vinegar until smooth. Stir in soy. Heat wok and add 1 tablespoon peanut oil. Stirfry pork 30 seconds. Add onions and ginger; stirfry 10 seconds. Add bamboo shoots, mushrooms, cabbage, green pepper and crab, separately and in order; stirfry 15 seconds each. Stir cornstarch mixture and add; cook and stir 1 minute. Stir in sesame oil. Remove and let cool completely. Place 1½ teaspoonsful mixture diagonally in center of won ton wrap and shape in ½'' x 2'' rectangle. Fold two sides over filling. Brush little egg at long end of wrapper. Roll up sealing on edge with egg. Heat peanut oil to 375° F. Carefully add egg rolls 3 to 4 at a time; frying to golden. Remove with slotted spoon and drain on paper towel. Serve hot.

Yield: about 3 dozen

Becky Karavatakis
Lafayette, La.

DIM SUM

3 med. dried black mushrooms,
  minced
1 t. cornstarch
1 t. cold water
2 t. soy sauce
2 t. rice vinegar
2 T. peanut oil
½ lb. lean ground pork
1 sm. egg, beaten

½ c. yellow onion,
  chopped fine
½ c. water chestnuts,
  chopped fine
2 t. curry powder
½ t. sugar
½ lb. won ton skins
4 c. peanut oil for frying

Mix cornstarch with water until smooth. Stir in vinegar and soy. Heat peanut oil in wok. Add meat; stirfry until lightly browned. Add onion; stirfry until clear. Add water chestnuts and mushrooms; stirfry about 45 seconds. Add curry; stirfry 20 seconds. Add cornstarch mixture and sugar; stirfry 30 seconds. Drain and cool. Trim won ton skins to circular shape (or leave square and make triangles). Place about 1½ teaspoonsful mixture in center. Fold over and crimp with fork. Lightly brush tops with egg. Heat oil in wok to 375° F. Fry 6 to 8 at a time, turning until golden. Remove with slotted spoon and drain on paper towel. Repeat making sure oil returns to 375° F. before adding additional batches. Serve hot.

Variations: 1) substitute chopped chicken and 2 T. sesame oil; 2) substitute chopped shrimp or crawfish and add 1 chopped Jalapeno pepper.

Yield: about 3 dozen

Becky Karavatakis
Lafayette, La.

PHYLLO PIES
TRIOPITA, SPANAKOPETES, BEEF PITAS, CRAWFISH PIES

½ lb. phyllo leaves
½ lb. melted butter

Choice of fillings

INDIVIDUAL TRIANGLES: cut phyllo into strips about 2" wide, the length of the pastry. Carefully brust the strip with melted butter. Place a scant teaspoonful filling at one end and fold over to form a triangle. Continue folding, as you would a flag, to the end of the strip. Repeat with remaining filling. May be frozen at this point. Bake at 375° F. for 8 to 10 minutes or until lightly golden brown. Serve hot.

BY THE TRAY: grease a 12 x 18 cookie sheet that has 1" sides. Remove one sheet of phyllo, place on cookie sheet and brush carefully with melted butter. Repeat one sheet at a time until 8 sheets have been stacked and buttered. Divide mixture into 3 equal parts. Carefully spread ⅓ of mixture over phyllo and top with 2 more buttered sheets. Spread next ⅓ mixture; top with 2 more buttered layers phyllo. Repeat procedure topping final portion with 6 buttered layers of phyllo. With a sharp knife score the top into rows about 1½" wide the length of the pan. Brush melted butter into the scores and around the edges of the pan. Bake at 350° F. for 30 minutes or until lightly golden brown. Cool and finish cutting into squares or diamond shapes.

Triopita/Cheese Pies
½ lb. Feta cheese, crumbled
½ lb. Ricotta cheese

2 lg. eggs, beaten
¼ t. Italian seasoning

Combine cheeses, seasonings, and eggs.

74

Spanakopetes/Spinach Pies

1 med. onion, chopped
¼ c. olive oil
2 10 oz. pkgs. frozen chopped spinach
⅓ lb. crumbled feta cheese

½ lb. dry cottage cheese
3 lg. eggs, beaten

Cook spinach; drain well. Saute onions in olive oil 5 minutes. Stir in spinach until dry; add cheeses and eggs.

Beef Pitas

2 T. olive oil
2 lg. onions, minced
¾ lb. lean ground round
2 lg. cloves garlic, pressed
2 lg. eggs, beaten
1 T. chili powder

1 t. cumin
½ t. turmeric
½ t. ginger
2 t. salt

Saute onions in oil. Add meat and seasonings; cook until meat is browned. Cool slightly; add eggs and mix well.

Mudbug Pitas/Crawfish Pies

1 lb. crawfish tails minced
1 lg. onions, minced
2 ribs celery, minced
3 T. olive oil

2 green onion tops, minced
1 clove garlic, minced
1 med. bell pepper, minced
Salt and pepper, to taste
2-3 dashes Tabasco

Saute vegetables in oil. Add crawfish; saute 5 minutes longer. Add seasonings to taste.

Yield: 7 to 8 dozen

Becky Karavatakis
Lafayette, La.

OYSTER TARTS

2 cans small smoked oysters
½ t. salt
1 lb. fresh spinach, trimmed
4 T. butter

1 lg. onion, minced
1 c. Half and Half
2 T. flour
48 unbaked Mini Tart
Shells (p.59)

Saute onion in 2 tablespoons butter for 5 minutes. Remove onions and reserve. Fry bacon in remaining butter until crisp. Remove; allow to cool and crumble. Reserve. Boil 1 cup water with salt. Add spinach and boil 1 minute. Drain and rinse under cold water. Drain and pat dry with towel. Chop fine. Reserve. Scald half and half over low heat. Reserve. Heat remaining butter over low heat until melted. Stir in flour to make a paste. Stir in half and half until smooth and mixture begins to thicken. Stir in onions, bacon and spinach. Spoon by teaspoonful into Mini Tart Shells and top with smoked oyster. Run under broiler just to heat oyster. Serve immediately.

Yield: 3 to 4 dozen

CHEESEBURGER TARTS

1 lb. ground round
2 lg. onions, minced
3 lg. eggs
48 unbaked Mini Tart Shells
   (p.59)

1½ c. cheddar, grated
1 can Rotel diced tomatoes
and green chillies
½ t. salt

Brown meat with onion and salt. Drain grease. Combine with eggs, tomatoes and chillies. Spoon into tart shells and top with grated cheese. Bake at 375° F. for 12 to 15 minutes or until cheese is melted and edge of crust begins to lightly brown.

Yield: 48

Becky Karavatakis
Lafayette, La.

SANDWICHES/CANAPES

CAJUN PETI FOURS

1 lb. loaf thin sliced
  firm bread (14 slices)
2 lb. loaf Velveeta cheese
  sliced in ⅛'' slices
1 lb. crawfish tails,
  minced
1 lg. onion, minced

1 bell pepper, seeded
and minced
1 rib celery, minced
2 T. butter
Tabasco
Salt and pepper
63 slices jalapeno pepper

Saute onions, bell pepper and celery in butter until soft. Add crawfish tails and continue cooking over low fire for 5 minutes. Season to taste with salt, pepper and Tabasco. Remove from heat. Trim crusts from bread; spread 7 slices of bread with mixture, and top with remaining seven slices. Cut each sandwich into nine squares and place on lightly greased baking sheet. Cover each square with 1 slice of cheese, and garnish with 1 slice of jalapeno pepper. Bake at 350° F. for 6 to 8 minutes or until cheese melted down around bread. Remove, let cool 3 to 5 minutes and serve warm.

Variations: 1) Use Mexican-style Velveeta, hot or mild; 2) for alligator or turtle filling: boil meat until tender with one onion, 2 ribs celery, 2 carrots and 1 clove garlic. Drain and grind meat. Reserve liquid and vegetables for soup; 3) For Italian Peti Four: spread bread with pizza sauce, sprinkle with Parmesan cheese; top with bread; cut into small circles with tall biscuit cutter and top with slice of pepperoni; cover with 2'' x 2'' slice of Mozzarella cheese, top with a pinch of Italian seasoning and if desired an anchovy rolled in a caper.

Yield: 63

Becky Karavatakis
Lafayette, La.

CORN PUPPIES

1 lb. cocktail wieners	1 lg. egg, beaten
⅔ c. yellow corn meal	Peanut oil
1 c. flour	Toothpicks
½ t. baking powder	½ t. salt
1 t. sugar	½ t. white pepper
2 T. oil	Hot Mustard (p. 21)
1 c. milk	Sweet 'N Sour Sauce (p. 22)

Heat peanut oil to 375° F. Mix corn meal, flour, baking powder, sugar and salt together. Add milk, oil and egg. Stir until smooth. Insert ½ toothpick into end of sausage. Dip into batter, covering entire sausage, and release slowly into hot oil. Cook until golden brown and drain on paper towels. Serve hot with Hot Mustard or Sweet 'N Sour Sauce.

Note: if cocktail wieners are not available or for a smoked taste use Hormel Little Smokie Sausages.

Variations: 1) for Cajun Corn Puppies add one minced onion, and 2 or 3 minced jalapenos to batter; and when the sausage is all gone add enough corn meal to make a thick batter and drop by teaspoonful into hot grease for some Cajun Style Hush Puppies; 2) for Cheese Puppies use 10 oz. any flavor Cracker Barrel cheese; cut in ½" x ½" cube-sticks the width of the cheese, follow instructions above.

Yield: 4 dozen

Becky Karavatakis
Lafayette, La.

CHEDDAR FLUFFS

6-oz. cream cheese
½ lb. Land of Lakes Country
   Morning Blend Marg., unsalted
½ lb. Kraft extra sharp
   cheddar cheese

1 t. dry mustard
4 lg. egg whites, stiffly
beaten
1 lg. loaf bread, crusts
cut off, cut in triangles

Melt cheeses, butter and mustard over low fire. Remove and cool. Gently fold in stiffly beaten egg whites just until blended. Dip bread into mixture, covering top and sides only. Place on parchment or waxed paper on cookie sheet and freeze. Can be transferred to plastic freezer bag until ready to use. Preheat oven to 400° F. and place bread on greased cookie sheet for about 10 minutes or until golden brown. Best served immediately.

Yield: 6 to 7 dozen

Dot Smith
Lafayette, La.

PUFF THE MAGIC CHICKEN

1 c. cooked chicken, minced
¼ c. celery, minced
½ t. lemon juice
Dash Tabasco

1 T. mayonnaise
¼ c. smoked almonds, chopped
Salt and pepper, to taste
60 La Petite Puff Shells (p. 65)

Mix chicken together with celery, lemon juice, mayonnaise, and almonds. Season to taste with Tabasco, salt and pepper. Split puff shells, fill and replace top. Serve cold or at room temperature.

Yield: 1½ c. filling
   about 60 puffs

Trudy Karavatakis
Lafayette, La.

PINWHEELS

Sliced bread,
   crusts removed
Philadelphia cream
   cheese, softened
Beau Monde seasoning

Stuffed green olives
Ripe olives, stuffed w/
   seasoned cream cheese
Small sweet gerkins
Small dill pickles

Season cream cheese with Beau Monde, to taste. (For special occasions, tint cheese with food coloring of your choice.) Spread on bread. Place choice of olives or pickles in a row at one edge of the bread. Roll up; wrap in plastic wrap and refrigerate until ready to serve. Remove and slice ¼'' thick.

Note: 1 slice of bread requires about 1-oz. of cream cheese for spreading and 6 olives or 2-3 pickles.

Yield: 12/slice

CHEESE WRAPS

1 lb. bacon, cut in
   half lengthwise
16 slices bread

8-oz. Velveeta cheese, room
   temperature

Trim crusts from bread and spread with cheese. Roll up; wrap on angle with bacon strip. Secure bacon ends with toothpicks. Run under broiler, turning once, until bacon is crisp (5 to 6 minutes).

Yield: 32

Gertrude Roesler Brown
Sunset, La.

FINGER SANDWICH LOAF

1 loaf unsliced firm bread
2-3 T. milk
Ham Filling

2 8-oz. pkg. cream cheese
Chicken Filling
Egg Filling

Trim crusts; slice lengthwise into 4 slices. Spread ham filling bottom slice. Add next slice; spread with chicken filling. Add next slice; spread with egg filling. Top with last slice. Wrap airtight; chill several hours. Beat cheese and milk until smooth. Spread half of mixture on top and sides of loaf. Decorate with remainder of cheese mixture with a #22 star tip thru a pastry bag. Garnish top with flower design made with vegetables. To serve cut in thirds lengthwise and slice ¾'' wide.

Ham Filling: Combine; cover and chill.
6-oz. thin sliced boiled
  ham, minced
¼ c. mayonnaise
¼ t. dry mustard

1 t. horseradish
2 T. sweet pickle
1 T. sweet relish
Salt and pepper, to taste

Chicken Filling: Combine; cover and chill.
1 whole chicken breast,
  cooked and minced
½ c. mayonnaise
2 T. minced celery

2 T. parsley, minced
½ t. lemon juice
Salt and pepper, to taste
2 T. chopped almonds

Egg Filling: Combine; cover and chill.
4 lg. boiled eggs, minced
½ t. minced onion
¼ c. mayonnaise

¼ t. salt
⅛ t. dill weed, minced
Dash dry mustard

Yield: about 3 dozen

Becky Karavatakis
Lafayette, La.

BAR-B-QUED HAMBURGER BITES

1 lb. lean ground round
1 med. onion, grated
1 lg. egg
1 t. Creole Mustard

1 t. Tony's seasoning
1 qt. BBQ sauce
36 Cocktail Buns

Combine meat, onion, egg, mustard and seasoning. Form into 1¼"
balls. Flatten slightly. Place on lightly greased cookie sheet and broil,
turning once until done.

Yield: about 36

MINI MUFFULETTAS

32 Mini Burger Buns (p.50)
Muffuletta Salad Mix
1 pkg. thin sliced salami

1 pkg. thin sliced pepperoni
1 pkg. sliced Provolone cheese

Spread Muffuletta Salad Mix on both sides of bun. Cut salami and
cheese with small round cutter. Put one slice each: pepperoni, salami
and cheese on bun.

Yield: 32

HAM AND CHEESE BUTTER HORNS

1 lb. thin sliced boiled ham
1 lb. Cambret or other soft cheese
1 recipe Irma's Swedish Butter Horn Rolls (p.49)

Split rolls and spread one side with cheese, and top with boiled ham.

*Yield: filling for about
6 dozen horns*

*Becky Karavatakis
Lafayette, La.*

BACON FINGERS

2 8-oz. pkg. cream cheese,
  softened
¼ c. milk
1 lb. bacon, cooked, drained,
  and crumbled
2 lg. loaves thin sliced bread

⅓ c. bell peppers,
  chopped fine
1 med. onion, minced
2 t. Worcestershire sauce
½ t. Italian seasoning
Salt and pepper, to taste

Blend cheese and milk until smooth. Add remaining ingredients and blend only until mixed. Trim crusts from bread and cut into thirds. Spread one side with mixture and top with second slice. Store between layers of wax paper in airtight container in refrigerator until ready to serve.

Yield: about 72

Becky Karavatakis
Lafayette, La.

PEANUT BUTTER FINGERS

1 sm. loaf sliced bread
1 c. creamy peanut butter
1 c. Wesson oil

1 t. garlic salt
1 t. paprika
¼ t. La. Hot Sauce

Trim crust from bread. Cut each slice into 7 strips. Toast crust and the bread strips until light brown in 300° F. oven. Crush bread crusts very find. Heat peanut butter, oil, garlic salt, paprika and Louisiana Hot Sauce until melted. Dip each bread strip into peanut butter mixture, drain and roll in bread crumbs. (Delicious with salads or cocktails.)

Yield: 7 to 8 dozen

Mildred Moench Tuten
Ruston, La.

MINI-RUBEN CANAPES

1 loaf party rye bread
1 c. Dijon mustard
¼ c. horseradish sauce
6 oz. pkg. sliced Swiss cheese

1 can sauerkraut, drained
1 can corned beef,
sliced thin

Combine mustard and horseradish. Spread on party rye and place on cookie sheet. Add a slice of corned beef and a teaspoon of sauerkraut. Top with a slice of Swiss cheese and broil, close to heat, until cheese melts and puffs — do not burn. Serve warm.

Yield: about 48

CHINESE SHRIMP TOAST

1 lb. shrimp, shelled, deveined
1 can water chestnuts
2 t. dry white wine
2 lg. eggs
¼ t. sugar
12 slices firm white bread

2 T. cornstarch
2 green onions with tops
1 T. gingerroot
¼ t. salt
1 c. oil for frying

Combine drained water chestnuts, gingerroot, salt, sugar and cornstarch in processor. Process to chunky. Add shrimp, wine, and onions. Process to mince shrimp. Trim crust from bread. Spread each slice with mixture and divide each slice into four strips. Heat oil in skillet to 375° F. Fry shrimp toast, spread side down for one minute turning to repeat on back side. Drain; cool on wire racks. Serve warm.

Yield: 4 dozen

*Becky Karavatakis
Lafayette, La.*

INDONESIAN CRAB POINTS

3 T. fresh lemon juice
1 clove garlic, minced
¼ c. roasted unsalted
   peanuts
1 T. peanut oil
¼ t. Tabasco
½ lb. crabmeat

½ c. mayonnaise
3 T. green onion tops,
   chopped fine
6 slices bread, toasted,
   cut into 4 triangles
2 T. parsley, minced
½ t. Tony's seasoning

Combine lemon, garlic, peanuts, oil and Tabasco in processor and blend until nuts are chopped fine, not smooth. Transfer to mixing bowl and add crab, mayonnaise, onion and Tony's seasoning. Spread about 1 tablespoon mixture on each toast point, place on baking sheet and bake in pre-heated oven at 450° F. for about 10 minutes, or until lightly browned on top. Top with a pinch of minced parsley.

Yield: 24

NOVA SCOTIA SALMON ROLLS

8 oz. pkg. cream cheese
½ c. onion puree
1 lb. smoked salmon, sliced

8 oz. Creole cream cheese
1 T. dill weed
1 t. Tabasco

Cream the cheeses with onion juice, dill weed and Tabasco. Cut the salmon into pieces about 2½ inches long. Spread each with cheese mixture and roll up. Put on cookie sheet, seam side down and place in freezer about 20 minutes. Remove and slice about ½″ thick slices. Serve on melba rounds.

Yield: 4 to 5 dozen

Becky Karavatakis
Lafayette, La.

SHRIMP RAFTS

1 lb. shrimp (31-35/lb.)
9 slices bread
6 green onions, w/tops
  chopped fine

3 lg. eggs
Salt and pepper, to taste
2½ c. peanut oil
½ c. cornstarch

Leave shell on tip of tail. Remove vein and cut half way through down the back of each shrimp. Press open and flatten out leaving tail tip standing up. Remove crust from bread and cut each slice in half. Cut each slice again lengthwise at slight angle leaving one end a little wider than the other. Beat eggs, cornstarch, salt and pepper. Dip each shrimp into egg mixture, making sure shrimp is completely coated and press gently into bread with tail part at the large end of the bread. Brush egg mixture over top of shrimp and bread. Sprinkle chopped onion down the center of shrimp and press lightly to cling. Repeat until all are ready to fry. Heat oil to 375° F. in wok or fry pan. Gently release into oil, top side up and cook 1 to 2 minutes on each side until golden. Drain top side. Serve warm.

Yield: 2½ to 3 dozen

Becky Karavatakis
Lafayette, La.

CRAB MELTAWAYS

7 oz. can crabmeat
7 oz. jar Old English
  sharp cheese
1 stick margarine

2 T. mayonnaise
½ t. seasoned salt
½ t. garlic powder
6 English muffins

Combine all ingredients, except muffins, and blend well. Spread on muffin halves and cut into quarters. Freeze at least 30 minutes. Broil and serve.

Yield: 48

Mrs. Bob Lott
Baltimore, Md.

PARTY RYE PIZZA

2 loaves party rye bread
1 lb. lean ground meat
1 lb. Owen's hot sausage

1 lb. Velveeta cheese
1 T. Worcestershire sauce

Brown ground meat and sausage. Drain off fat. Cut cheese into small pieces and mix with ground meat and heat until cheese melts. Stir in Worcestershire sauce. DO NOT ADD SALT. Spread 1 teaspoonful on each slice of rye bread. Place on cookie sheet and freeze. Transfer to freezer bag or container. Heat on cookie sheet at 350° F. about 15 minutes before serving.

Yield: about 6 dozen

Alice Eastin
Lafayette, La.

PIZZA DOLLARS

⅓ c. olive oil
½ t. garlic powder
15 oz. can tomato sauce
1 med. onion, minced fine
1 bell pepper, minced fine
1 t. Italian seasoning
Dash red pepper

8 oz. mozzarella cheese
grated
8 oz. Fontina cheese,
grated
4 oz. Parmesan cheese,
grated
Pizza Dough Rounds

Saute onion and bell pepper in oil until softened. Stir in garlic powder, Italian seasoning, and pepper. Mix cheeses together. Place Pizza Dough Rounds on greased baking sheet. Press each round in center to slightly raise outer edge. Spread tomato sauce on evenly. Top with small amount of onion mixture. Cover with grated cheeses and top with slice of pepperoni, etc. Bake in 425° F. oven for about 10 minutes or until crust is golden brown and top is bubbly.

Yield: about 8 dozen

Becky Karavatakis
Lafayette, La.

PIZZA DOUGH ROUNDS

3 c. flour
1 pkg. active dry yeast
¾ c. warm water

2 T. olive oil
1 T. honey
1 t. salt

Process flour and dry yeast together. Combine liquids in small bowl; slowly add to flour mixture while motor is running to form a ball. (Add a little extra water if necessary to form ball.) Knead on floured board until smooth, about ten minutes. Place in greased bowl, turning to coat all sides. Let rest, covered, with damp towel 30 to 45 minutes at room temperature. Break about 1 rounded teaspoon of dough and roll into balls. Press to flatten with bottom of glass dusted in flour. Refrigerate, covered, between layers of waxed paper until ready to use.

Yield: about 8 dozen

Becky Karavatakis
Lafayette, La.

JOSEFINAS

8 hard rolls or 1 thin loaf
    French bread
1 c. canned green chilies
1 c. butter

1 clove garlic, minced
1 c. mayonnaise
8 oz. Monterry Jack
    cheese, grated

Slice rolls or bread into ½" slices. Toast on one side. Rinse seeds off chilies and chop. Mix chilies with butter and garlic. Spread the chili mixture on the untoasted sides of bread slices. Mix mayonnaise and cheese. Spread on bread. Broil until cheese is brown and puffy. Serve at once.

Yield: about 30

Daryl Hause Tanner
Corpus Christi, Tx.

BRUNCH BISCUITS

1 dozen lg. eggs
¼ c. milk
¼ c. butter

1 batch Ham Biscuits
1 batch Bacon Biscuits

Beat eggs with milk until fluffy. Heat butter in skiller until melted. Add eggs and soft scramble. Remove to heated dish. Serve as a filling with Ham Biscuits and Bacon Biscuits.

Ham Biscuits
2 c flour
2 T. butter
4 t. baking powder

½ c. ham (95-97% fat free)
ground or minced fine
¾ c. milk

Sift flour with salt and baking powder. Place ham in mixing bowl and sift flour mixture over ham. Cut in butter. Add milk and mix only until blended. (I sift right into bowl of food processor and process 15 to 20 seconds.) Roll out on flour board and cut out with small glass or 1½" cutter. Bake on greased baking sheet at 400° F. until tops are golden, about 8 minutes. Makes about 30.

Variations: add ¼ c. onion and/or ¼ c. grated cheese.

Bacon Biscuits
2 c. flour
2 T. bacon drippings
4 t. baking powder

½ lb. bacon, crisp,
crumbled
¾ c. milk

Prepare as above.

Variations: add ¼ c. onion and 1 med. minced jalapeno.

Yield: about 60

Becky Karavatakis
Lafayette, La.

MOLDS/SPREADS

PARTY CHEESE BALL

9 oz. sharp cheddar cheese
   grated
6 oz. hot pepper cheese,
   grated
8 oz. soft cream cheese

1 med. onion, grated
1 T. Worcestershire
   sauce
1 lg. bell pepper
   chopped fine

Have all cheeses at room temperature. Mix ingredients with electric mixer. Chill at least 1 hour; form into ball or log. Roll in a mixture of crushed crackers and parsley flakes. Serve with your choice of crackers.

Yield: about 3 cups

Unna P. Kukla
Houston, Tx.

THE NOW FAMOUS CHEESE RING

1 lb. sharp cheddar, grated
1 c. pecans, chopped
¾ c. Hellmann's mayonnaise
4 green onions w/tops, chopped

1 clove garlic, pressed
½ t. Tabasco
1 c. strawberry preserves

Combine all ingredients, except preserves, and mix well. Grease ring mold with Pam or other oil. Put mixture in mold and chill until set. Unmold onto a platter and fill center with preserves. Serve with Keebler Townhouse crackers.

Yield: 1 quart

Jennifer Badalamenti
New Orleans, La.

GARLIC CHEESE BALL

8-oz. Philadelphia cream cheese
10-oz. sharp cheese, grated
4 T. butter

2 lg. cloves garlic,
pressed
Parsley or paprika

Bring to room temperature. Combine butter, cheeses, and garlic. Roll to ball or other desired shape. Wrap and refrigerate at least 4 hours. Garnish with parsley or paprika.

Yield: 2¼ cups

Alice Eastin
Lafayette, La.

CHRISTMAS MOUSSE

10 oz. pkg. frozen chopped
spinach, drained uncooked
8 oz. cottage cheese, drained
2 ribs celery, diced small
2 green onions, with tops
chopped fine
½ c. mayonnaise

1 t. unflavored gelatin
½ c. ice water
1 sm. pkg. lemon jello
1 c. boiling water
Salt and pepper, to taste
1½ t. cider vinegar

Dissolve gelatin and Jello in hot water. Add water; beat in mayonnaise and vinegar. Season to taste. Refrigerate until set. Beat with electric mixer until slightly fluffy. Add remaining ingredients and mix well. Pour into greased Christmas tree or wreath mold; chill until firm. Garnish with cherry tomatoes and almond slices.

Variations: 1) for a Greek taste, try 4 oz. feta cheese and 4 oz. Ricotta cheese, adding a dash of garlic and oregano; 2) use frozen chopped broccoli in place of spinach.

Yield: 1 quart mold

Becky Karavatakis
Lafayette, La.

''TIPSY'' CHEESE BALL

½ c. chopped dried apricots
¼ c. raisins
1 lb. mild cheddar cheese
½ c. toasted pecans, chopped

¼ c. bourbon
8 oz. pkg. cream cheese,
softened
¼ c. chopped dates

Combine apricots and liquor; let stand at least one hour. Blend cheeses; stir in apricots with liquor, pecans, dates and raisins. Blend thoroughly. Shape into ball and chill until firm. Roll in parsley or pecans and chill until ready to serve. Garnish with pecan halves. Serve with assorted crackers or thin breads.

Yield: 1 2-lb. ball or
    2 1-lb. balls

Jane Breaux
Lafayette, La.

HOLIDAY CHEESE BALL

2 8-oz. pkg. cream cheese
1 8½-oz. can crushed
  pineapple
¼ c. green bell pepper,
  chopped fine

1 sm. onion, chopped fine
1 T. seasoned salt
1½ c. pecans, chopped

Mix together and shape into ball. Garnish as desired. Wrap tightly and refrigerate until ready to serve.

Yield: 1 large ball or
    2 small balls

Kathleen Esteb
Baton Rouge, La.

SUSAN'S CHEESE MOLD

4 oz. blue cheese, crumbled
8 oz. cheddar cheese, shredded
3 oz. pkg. cream cheese, softened
1 c. chopped pecans (optional)

2 T. onion, finely
chopped
½ c. sour cream

Blend all ingredients together well. Rub a 3 to 4 cup mold with butter or mayonnaise. Pat cheese into mold. Chill until firm. Place serving plate or tray on top of mold and turn over quickly. Garnish with items of your choice. Serve with assorted crackers.

Yield: about 3 cups

Susan Harrison
Lafayette, La.

SHRIMP CHEESE BALL

1 lb. boiled shrimp, peeled
1 bunch green onions, chopped
Juice of 1 lemon
¼ t. Accent (MSG)
Dash of Worcestershire sauce

2 8-oz. pkg. cream cheese
2 cloves garlic, minced
⅛ t. red pepper (or to
taste)
1 c. fine chopped pecans

Combine shrimp, green onions, lemon juice, pepper, garlic and Accent in a food processor using steel blades. Process until finely chopped. Add cream cheese and blend. Chill until firm. Separate into 2 or 3 balls (will be soft). Roll in pecans. Chill.

Yield: about 4 cups

Midge Scardina
Baton Rouge, La.

SHRIMP LOAF

1 c. tomato soup
3 sm. pkg. cream cheese
1½ T. unflavored gelatin
2 cans medium shrimp, crumbled

1 c. mayonnaise
¾ c. celery, chopped
¼ c. onions, minced
Salt and pepper, to taste

Soak gelatin in ¼ c. cold water. Heat soup to boiling. Dissolve cream cheese in soup. Add gelatin. Cool. Add mayonnaise, celery, onions and seasoning to taste. When mixture begins to thicken, add crumbled shrimp. Pour in greased mold and chill until set. Serve with crackers.

Note: For crab loaf, substitute 2 cans crab, flaked. K.B.

Yield: about 4½ cups

Kim Bergeron
Lafayette, La.

SHRIMP MOLD

1 can Campbell's Tomato Soup
8-oz. Philadelphia Cream
   cheese, softened
1 pkg. Knox unflavored gelatin
1 c. mayonnaise

¾ c. chopped celery
¾ c. chopped green onion
6-8 drops Tabasco
2 lbs. boiled shrimp

Peel and chop shrimp. Heat soup until boiling just a bit. Add cream cheese. Stir until cheese is melted and well blended with soup. Dissolve 2 tablespoons of soup mixture with gelatin, until it is a paste consistency. Mix all ingredients together. Pour mixture into greased mold. Refrigerate overnight. Serve with crackers.

Yield: about 8 cups

Thelma Moser
Gretna, La.

SALMON PARTY BALL

2 c. salmon (cooked) or
   1 lg. can
1 8-oz. cream cheese
1 T. + 1 t. lemon juice
2 t. grated onion
2½ t. horseradish

¼ t. salt
¼ t. liquid smoke
½ c. pecans, chopped
   fine
3 T. snipped parsley

Drain and flake salmon. Beat cream cheese, lemon juice, onion, horseradish, salt and liquid smoke. Mix thoroughly with salmon. Chill several hours. Combine pecans and parsley. Shape into 3 small balls or 1 large and roll in nut mixture. Wrap in saran wrap. Freezes well up to 6 weeks. Serve with crackers (delicious with Triscuits).

Yield: about 3¼ cups

Unna P. Kukla
Houston, Texas

TUNA MOLD

8 oz. cream cheese, softened
2 T. chili sauce
2 T. parsley

1 T. minced onion
½ t. Tabasco
2 7-oz. cans white tuna,
   drained and flaked

Blend cream cheese, chili sauce, parsley, onion and Tabasco. Add tuna and mix well. Pack firmly in 1 quart mold, well greased with mayonnaise. Chill 4 hours. Unmold and serve with crackers or celery sticks for stuffing.

Yield: about 4 cups

Becky Karavatakis
Lafayette, La.

97

OYSTER PATE

2 8-oz. pkgs. cream cheese,
  softened
¼ c. half and half
2 cans smoked oysters, minced
Paprika

1 T. lemon juice
1 T. Worcestershire
2½ T. mayonnaise
1 T. parsley, chopped
1-2 dashes Tabasco sauce

Blend cream cheese with cream. Add mayonnaise, oysters, lemon juice, Worcestershire and Tabasco sauce. Mix together. Shape into block, smooth with knife. Wrap airtight and chill until ready to serve. Sprinkle top with parsley and paprika. Serve with crackers or melba toast.

Yield: about 3 cups

Becky Karavatakis
Lafayette, La.

CRABMEAT MOLD

8 oz. cream cheese
2 c. grated onion
10 oz. cream of mushroom
  soup, undiluted
1 c. mayonnaise

1 T. gelatin, dissolved in
3 T. water
1 lb. fresh crabmeat
1 c. chopped celery

Soften gelatin in water. Heat soup. Add gelatin mixture, stir until dissolved. Cool slightly. Combine with other ingredients. Pour into large, well greased, Tupperware mold. Chill several hours or overnight.

Yield: about 8 cups

Peggy Meaux
Lafayette, La.

SALMON SPREAD

1 8-oz. can salmon
8 oz. cream cheese
2 green onions w/tops,
   chopped fine

¼ t. paprika
Dash Tabasco
Dash salt
½ t. dill weed

Flake salmon. Using a fork combine all ingredients. Form into desired shape and refrigerate 1 to 2 hours.

Variation: For dip: add ¼ c. Half and Half cream and process ingredients until smooth. This makes about 2 cups.

Yield: 1¾ cups

AVOCADO MOUSSE

1 env. unflavored gelatin
1 c. cold chicken broth
½ t. Tony's seasoning
1½ c. avocado, mashed
½ c. sour cream

¼ c. green onion tops,
   chopped fine
Juice of 1 lemon
½ t. Tabasco

Soften gelatin in cold chicken broth in a small saucepan for about 1 minute. Add Tony's and stir over medium heat until dissolved. Reserve. Combine avocado, sour cream, green onion, lemon juice and Tabasco. Stir in gelatin. Pour into a well greased 3 cup ring mold and refrigerate until firm. Unmold onto serving platter and garnish with parsley, divided cherry tomatoes and strips of pimento.

Yield: about 2¾ cup

Becky Karavatakis
Lafayette, La.

HAM MOUSSE

2 chicken livers
2 T. unsalted butter
1 ¼ t. unflavored gelatin
½ c. boiled ham
Sprigs of parsley

2 oz. cold chicken stock
2 oz. smoked ham, minced
½ c. heavy cream
½ c. sliced smoked
almonds

Clean liver; cut in half. Melt butter over medium high heat. Cook liver until browned outside, but still pink inside, about 3 minutes. Drain. Sprinkle gelatin over stock in skillet and let stand until softened. Heat over medium heat, stirring constantly until dissolved. Combine meats; process until smooth. Continue processing; add cream and gelatin mixture. Process until smooth. Pour mixture into a 3 cup greased mold; chill at least 4 hours. Turn out on platter lined with lettuce; garnish with almonds and parsley. Serve with sliced rye bread and small slices of swiss cheese.

Yield: about 3 cups

ORIENTAL CHEESE SPREAD

8 oz. pkg. cream cheese
½ t. ground ginger

1 ½ T. light soy
¼ c. sesame seeds

Toast sesame seeds for about 10 minutes in 300° F. oven, stirring every 2 to 3 minutes. Let cool. Combine all ingredients and blend well. Form into shape desired; wrap in plastic wrap and chill. Serve with melba rounds.

Variation: use 8 1-oz. square slices ham. Spread about 1 ounce mixture on each slice. Roll up. Chill. Slice about ½" thick. Makes about 96.

Yield: about ¾ cup

Becky Karavatakis
Lafayette, La.

POLYNESIAN SPREAD

2 8-oz. pkgs. cream cheese,
  softened
1 fresh pineapple, crushed or
  1 8½-oz. can, crushed
2 sm. green onion w/tops,
  chopped fine

¼ c. chopped green
  peppers
⅓ c. macadamia nut bits
  or chopped pecans
1 t. Tony's seasoning

Combine in processor or blender until mixed, but not smooth. Cover and chill 3-4 hours or overnight. Serve in hollowed out pineapple half with crackers.

Yield: about 1½ cups

MOCK CRAB SPREAD

2 14-oz. cans artichokes
  hearts, rinsed and drained
2 c. Hellmann's mayonnaise
½ t. lemon juice

1 T. Italian seasoning
¼ t. garlic powder
¼ t. onion powder
Salt and pepper, to taste

Combine all ingredients in blender or processor. Carefully combine until mixed, but leaving artichokes chunky. Refrigerate. Heat through. Serve hot with crackers.

Yield: about 3½ cups

Becky Karavatakis
Lafayette, La.

ENGLISH STYLE POTTED SHRIMP

2 6¼-oz. cans shrimp,
  extra small size, rinsed
¼ t. mace
½ t. garlic puree
1 t. lemon juice

½ t. dill weed
⅛ t. dry mustard
⅛ t. salt
Dash black pepper
6 T. butter

Bring butter to room temperature. Puree remaining ingredients in blender. Stir in butter. Chill, covered, overnight.

Yield: 1⅔ cups

Becky Karavatakis
Lafayette, La.

BRAUNSCHWEIGER SPREAD

½ lb. Braunschweiger, cubed
¼ med. onion, quartered
¼ c. celery
¼ c. sweet pickle relish

⅛ t. Tabasco
2 T. sweet pickle
juice
2 sprigs parsley, chopped

Combine in blender or processor. Blend until smooth.

Yield: 1¾ cup

Thelma Moser
Gretna, La.

CORNED BEEF SPREAD

1 sm. can corned beef, chopped
1 sm. onion, grated
3 T. sweet pickle relish

1 T. horseradish
2 T. mayonnaise
½ t. lemon juice

Combine and chill. Serve with crackers or vegetable sticks.

Yield: about 1¾ cups

Becky Karavatakis
Lafayette, La.

DEVILED EGG SPREAD

6 lg. eggs, hard boiled,
  chopped fine
3 T. mayonnaise
1½ t. Creole mustard
¼ t. onion powder
¼ t. red pepper
⅛ t. oregano
Salt to taste

3 ribs celery, minced
3-oz. pkg. Cream cheese,
  softened
1½ T. milk or cream
Small jar pimiento-stuffed
  olives, sliced
Small can sliced ripe olives
Paprika

Mix eggs, celery, mayonnaise, mustard, onion, salt, pepper and oregano until blended. Shape onto lined serving platter, smoothing edges. Cover gently and refrigerate at least two hours.

Yield: about 2¼ cups

Becky Karavatakis
Lafayette, La.

PIMENTO CHEESE SPREAD

1 lb. extra sharp cheddar
4-oz. diced pimentos,
  drained
¾ c. fine chopped pecans
½ c. mayonnaise
12 pimento stuffed olives, diced

2 T. dry white wine
1 T. olive juice
1 t. sugar
½ t. pepper
½ t. Tabasco

Combine and chill.

Yield: about 4 cups

Sharron Brown Mayers
Baton Rouge, La.

BACON AND PECAN SPREAD

4 thick slices bacon, cooked,
  drained and crumbled
1 c. sour cream
8 oz. pkg. cream cheese,
  softened
1 t. dried parsley

1 medium onion, minced
  fine
2 ribs celery, minced fine
¼ c. pecans, chopped
½ t. salt

Combine all ingredients, except parsley, and blend. Shape into loaf and sprinkle top with parsley. Chill. Serve with Triscuits, celery, or as a spread for finger sandwiches.

Yield: about 2½ cups

MICRO-BRIE WITH ALMOND BUTTER

1 can Danish Brie
2 T. unsalted butter
2 T. blanched sliced almonds

Combine butter and almonds in glass bowl; microwave on high 3½ minutes. Spoon over cheese and microwave on medium-high or 70% power until cheese is hot, about 1 to 1½ minutes. Serve as a spread for crackers.

Yield: about 1 cup

Becky Karavatakis
Lafayette, La.

104

MUSHROOM SPREAD

¾ c. fresh mushrooms
¼ c. plain yogurt
3 oz. pkg. cream cheese

1 sm. onion, minced
½ t. Tony's seasoning

Process and chill overnight. Keep refrigerated until ready to serve.
Serve with crackers.

Yield: 1¼ cups.

Becky Karavatakis
Lafayette, La.

CREAM CHEESE AND OLIVE SPREAD

6 oz. cream cheese, softened
2 T. mayonnaise
½ c. pimento stuffed
  olives, chopped

4 green onions, w/tops
sliced thin
⅛ t. red pepper

Combine and chill. Great for stuffing celery or cherry tomatoes or as
a sandwich spread.

Yield: about 1¼ cups

Becky Karavatakis
Lafayette, La.

DILLED CREAM CHEESE

3 oz. Philadelphia cream
  cheese, softened
½ t. mustard

½ t. dried dill weed
1 T. butter

Mix all ingredients together and form a ball. Roll in parsley or fine
chopped pecans, or sprinkle with paprika. Serve as a spread for sandwiches, crackers, or vegetables.

Yield: about 3½ oz.

Kathleen Esteb
Baton Rouge, La.

COLD DIPS

TEX-MEX LAYERED DIP

15 oz. can refried beans
2 c. sour cream
1¼ oz. pkg. taco seasoning
8 oz. jar picante sauce
4 ripe avocadoes, mashed
2 t. lemon or lime juice

2 med. tomatoes, chopped
bunch green onions, with
tops, thinly sliced
8 oz. cheddar cheese, grated
4 oz. can ripe olives,
sliced

Spread refried beans on bottom of 2 quart glass bowl. Mix sour cream and taco seasoning; spread on top of bean layer. Layer picante sauce next. Spread avocadoes mixed with lemon or lime juice. Continue layering each of the next ingredients. Cover with plastic wrap and refrigerate. Serve chilled with tostados or tortilla chips.

Yield: about 2 quarts

Daryl Hause Tanner
Corpus Christi, Tx.

TEX-MEX DIP

3 med. avocados
2 T. lemon juice
½ t. salt
¼ t. pepper
1 c. sour cream
½ c. mayonnaise

1 pkg. taco seasoning mix
2 10½ oz. cans jalapeno bean dip
1 bunch green onions w/tops chopped (1 cup)
3 med. tomatoes, seeded & coarsely chopped
2 3½-oz. can ripe olives, chopped
8 oz. pkg. sharp cheddar, grated

Mash avocados in medium size bowl with lemon juice, salt and pepper. Combine sour cream, mayonnaise and taco seasoning in small bowl. To assemble in 6 x 10 x 2" dish, spread bean dip, top with avocado mix, layer with sour cream-taco mix. Sprinkle with onions, tomatoes, and olives. Top with cheese.

Yield: about 3½ pints

Francie Ellis
Lafayette, La.

GUACA "MEAUX" LE

2 ripe avocados, mashed
   reserve 1 seed
2 T. grated onion
Juice of 1 lemon
Salt and pepper, to taste

½ tomato, peeled and chopped
   fine
½ t. cilantro or coriander
½ T. Tabasco or to taste

Combine ingredients and blend well. Place the avocado seed in the mixture and cover tightly to prevent mixture from turning brown. Refrigerate until ready to use.

Yield: 1½ to 2 cups

Sharron Brown Mayers
Baton Rouge, La.

GUACAMOLE DIP

2 med. California Avocados
½ c. sour cream
2 T. fine chopped onions
2 T. lemon juice

2 T. rice vinegar
2 t. Worcestershire
1 t. garlic salt
1-2 dashes Tabasco

Process until smooth and creamy. Serve with corn chips or as a filling for celery or cherry tomatoes.

Yield: about 2 cups

Becky Karavatakis
Lafayette, La.

CHILI CON QUESO DIP

2 lb. Velveeta cheese,
  cubed
1 lb. lean ground round
1 lb. yellow onion, minced

2 t. chili powder
2 10½-oz. cans Rotel
tomatoes and green chilies,
cut up
2 T. Picante Sauce (p. 20)

Saute onions in butter for 5 minutes, reserve. Brown ground meat and drain. Melt cheese over double boiler; stir in meat, onions, chili powder, and Rotel tomatoes. For zesty dip stir in Picante Sauce.

Yield: about 2 quarts

Becky Karavatakis
Lafayette, La.

CHEESE JALAPENO DIP

1 qt. mayonnaise
1 lb. Velveeta cheese,
  grated

8-oz. jar jalapeno peppers
1 lg. onion, chopped

Put ½″ water in blender. Add onions and jalapenos; blend together. Drain. Mix with remaining ingredients. For a thicker dip, add cream cheese to desired consistency.

Yield: about ½ gallon

Kim Bergeron
Lafayette, La.

OYSTER DIP

8-oz. Philadelphia cream cheese
1 can smoked oysters, drained,
   minced
1 sm. can chopped ripe olives

3 T. lemon juice
1 c. Hellmann's mayonnaise
5 or more drops Tabasco

Mix well. Chill at least one hour. Serve with Waverly wafers or Wheat thins.

Yield: 2 cups

Vivian Mays
Lafayette, La.

ANCHOVY DIP

½ t. garlic puree
½ t. dry mustard
1 t. Worcestershire sauce
1 T. anchovy paste
½ c. sour cream

3 T. green onions
3 T. wine vinegar
1 c. mayonnaise
3 T. parsley flakes
Dash black pepper

Process or blend. Chill. Serve with artichoke quarters, asparagus spears, or hearts of palm.

Yield: about 2 cups

Becky Karavatakis
Lafayette, La.

SARDINE DIP

2 sm. cans sardines
2 3-oz. pkg. cream cheese
⅓ c. onion minced (med.)
1 t. lemon juice

1 clove garlic, minced
2 T. Worcestershire
Dash pepper

Remove bone from sardines. Combine with remaining ingredients and process on and off until blended but not smooth. Chill at least an hour before serving.

Variation: Try smoked oysters or smoked clams.

Yield: about 2 cups

Becky Karavatakis
Lafayette, La.

CLAM DIP

2 8-oz. pkg. Philadelphia
  cream cheese, softened
1 can minced clams w/juice

1 T. Worcestershire sauce
1½ T. grated onion
½ t. Tabasco sauce

Combine ½ clam juice with remaining ingredients. Thin to desired consistency with remaining juice. Cover and refrigerate at least one hour or overnight.

Yield: about 3½ cups

Helen G. Aertker
Baton Rouge, La.

SHRIMP DIP I

2 4-oz. cans small shrimp
1 c. mayonnaise
4 T. grated onion

1 t. Tabasco sauce
Salt and pepper, to taste
Optional: sour cream

Mince shrimp; add mayonnaise, onions, Tabasco sauce, salt and pepper. Thin with sour cream, if desired. Serve with chips or crackers.

Yield: about 2 cups

Jane Breaux
Lafayette, La.

SHRIMP DIP II

4½ oz. can shrimp, broken
3 oz. pkg. cream cheese, softened
Dash of lemon juice

½ c. mayonnaise
½ c. onion,
chopped fine

Combine ingredients and mix well with an electric mixer. Chill several hours. This recipe doubles or triples well. Serve with crackers or vegetables. Keep in refrigerator until ready to use.

Yield: about 1½ cups

Lu Hardeman
Lafayette, La.

TARAMASALATA
FISH ROE DIP

3 oz. jar or fresh fish roe
1 sm. onion, chopped fine
1½ c. olive oil

1 c. potatoes, boiled,
peeled and mashed
Juice of 2 lemons

Mash roe and grated onion. Add a little oil and beat to form a paste. Continue beating and add potato, oil, and lemon and beat until nice paste of consistent color. Serve as a dip for seafood, or a spread for crackers.

Yield: about 2 cups

Erifili Eleftheriadis
Skopelos, Greece

BROCCOLI AND CRAB DIP

8-oz. pkg. broccoli,
frozen, chopped
6-oz. lump crabmeat
1 c. mayonnaise
1 T. lemon juice
½ t. salt

¼ c. green onions
chopped fine
¼ onions, chopped fine
1 c. parsley, chopped
1 t. dill weed

Thaw broccoli and drain between paper towels. Combine all ingredients and mix well. Cover and chill at least one hour. Serve cold with platter of assorted vegetables and crackers for dipping.

Variation: omit mayonnaise. Add 2-oz. softened cream cheese. Blend and stuff mushroom caps. Broil until bubbly. Serve hot.

Yield: about 3 cups

Sharron Brown Mayers
Baton Rouge, La.

IMAM BAILDI MEZE
EGGPLANT DIP

1 sm. eggplant
Salt
1 c. olive oil
2 lg. onions, minced
3 lg. tomatoes, peeled
   and chopped

3 sm. cloves garlic
Parsley, chopped
Salt and pepper
½ c. water
6 green olives, sliced
1 T. capers

Pare eggplant, leaving alternate strips one inch wide with the skin on. Slice ½" thick. Sprinkle eggplant with salt. Let set for 10 minutes. Brown eggplant in ½ cup of olive oil, turning to brown all sides. Drain and chop. Combine with remaining oil, onions, tomatoes, garlic, parsley and ½ cup water. Bring to boil, cover and simmer about 40 minutes. Let cool. Spoon into serving dish and garnish with sliced olives and capers. Serve with onion or garlic crackers.

Yield: about 1½ cups

Becky Karavatakis
Lafayette, La.

ZUCCHINI DIP

8-oz. pkg. Philadelphia cream
   cheese, softened
2 T. Hellmann's mayonnaise
½ c. grated zucchini

¼ t. lemon juice
2 T. fine slivered
   toasted almonds
¼ t. Beau Monde seasoning

Cream cheese and mayonnaise together with Beau Monde and lemon juice until smooth. Stir in zucchini and almonds. Cover and refrigerate at least one hour. Serve with bread sticks or vegetables for dipping.

Yield: 1½ cups

Sharron B. Mayers
Baton Rouge, La.

VEGETABLE DIP WITH BREAD

1 round loaf white bread,
   hollowed out with center
   and cut into pieces
1 pkg. chopped frozen spinach,
   cooked, and drained dry
1 can water chestnuts, chopped
   fine

½ c. mayonnaise
1 c. sour cream
4 green onions w/tops,
   chopped fine
1 pkg. dried Knorr's
   vegetable soup mix

Reserve bread. Combine remaining ingredients. Place in hollowed out bread. Surround with bread pieces for dipping.

Yield: about 3 cups

Kathleen Esteb
Baton Rouge, La.

SPINACH DIP

1 10-oz. pkg. frozen chopped
   spinach, cooked and drained
1 pkg. Knorr's vegetable
   soup mix
½ small onion, chopped fine

¾ c. mayonnaise
1 c. sour cream
1 can water chestnuts,
   chopped

Combine all ingredients and mix well. Store in refrigerator overnight. Stir several times before serving.

Note: Serve in hollowed out bread loaf. Surround with bread pieces for dipping. Kathleen Esteb.

Yield: about 3 cups

Valerie Gonzalez
Baton Rouge, La.

DAFFODIL DIP

½ c. mayonnaise
8-oz. cream cheese
1 lg. hard boiled egg
2 T. chopped onion

2 T. fresh chopped parsley
1 clove garlic, minced
1 T. anchovy paste
Black pepper to taste

Combine mayonnaise to softened cream cheese. Add parsley, chopped egg white, onion, garlic and anchovy. Mix together. Crumble yolk and sprinkle on top. Serve from hollowed out cabbage surrounded with fresh vegetables. (Celery, radishes, cucumbers, cherry tomatoes, carrot sticks and cauliflower).

Yield: 2 cups

Phyllis Seal
Houston, Texas

DEVILED DIP

4 lg. boiled eggs
3-oz. cream cheese
1 T. milk
¼ c. mayonnaise

1 t. mustard
¼ t. horseradish
2 scallion tops, chopped
Salt and pepper, to taste

Process until blended, but not smooth. Place in bowl, garnish with parsley and paprika. Surround with raw vegetables for dipping.

Yield: about 1½ cups

Becky Karavatakis
Lafayette, La.

HEART HEALTHY CHILI SAUCE DIP

1 12-oz. bottle chili sauce
2 T. fresh lemon juice
3-4 drops Tabasco sauce
1 T. minced parsley

2 T. horseradish
¼ c. fine chopped celery

Combine all ingredients and chill. Serve with crisp raw vegetables.

Yield: 1¾ cups

Vivian Mays
Lafayette, La.

HORSERADISH DIP

8 oz. cream cheese, softened
8 oz. sour cream

2 T. horseradish
2 t. dried parsley

Cream the horseradish into the cream cheese. Stir in the sour cream. Chill for at least 2 hours. Garnish top with parsley. Serve as a dip for vegetables or crabfingers.

Yield: 1 pint

Becky Karavatakis
Lafayette, La.

ROQUEFORT DIP

4-oz. Roquefort cheese, crumbled
1 lb. Creole cream cheese
½ tsp. garlic powder, optional

½ c. sour cream
1 sm. onion, minced

Process and chill several hours. Serve with crackers.

Yield: about 2½ cups

Becky Karavatakis
Lafayette, La.

VEGETABLES CURRY

8 oz. sour cream
8 oz. cream cheese, softened
1 T. green onion tops,
   minced fine
1 T. parsley, minced

2 t. soy sauce
1 t. white rice vinegar
1 t. dillweed
1 t. curry powder
¼ c. Half and Half cream

Blend cheeses together. Add all other ingredients together except cream. Add enough cream to give good dipping consistency. Blend well. Chill at least 1 hour. Serve from a scooped out red cabbage surrounded with your favorite vegetables for dipping.

Variation: serve from cantaloupe with melon balls.

Yield: 2 cups

CURRIED MUSTARD DIP

1 c. mayonnaise
¼ c. Creole mustard
1 t. Italian seasoning
¼ t. plus a dash, curry
Salt and white pepper, to taste

1 T. fresh chopped parsley
1 T. dry minced onion
½ t. lemon juice
½ t. Worcestershire sauce

Combine all ingredients until well blended. Cover and chill at least 2 hours. Serve with favorite vegetables or seafood.

Yield: 1½ to 1¾ cups

Becky Karavatakis
Lafayette, La.

AVOCADO AND BACON DIP

1 ripe avocado
2 t. lemon juice
¼ c. sour cream
1 t. minced onion

¼ t. garlic salt
¼ t. paprika
¼ c. crumbled bacon

Peel, pit and mash avocado. Add remaining ingredients. Cover tightly; refrigerate until ready to serve.

Yield: 1¼ cup

Celia Pope
Baton Rouge, La.

BACON DIP

4 to 6 slices of bacon
8 oz. carton sour cream

1 T. horseradish
1 t. Worcestershire sauce

Cook bacon until crisp; drain and crumble. Combine all ingredients. Serve as a dip or as a spread on crackers.

Yield: 1 cup

Celia Pope
Baton Rouge, La.

BEAN AND BACON DIP

8 oz. can refried beans
8 oz. sour cream
4 slices bacon, crumbled
1 T. reserved bacon fat

1 med. onion minced
¼ t. garlic powder
Salt and pepper, to taste
1-2 dashes Tabasco

Saute onions in fat until soft. Add beans; stir over low heat until hot. Add seasonings and sour cream; fold in bacon. Chill.

Yield: about 2 cups

Becky Karavatakis
Lafayette, La.

VEGETABLE DIP I

1 pt. Hellmann's mayonnaise
8 oz. sour cream
½ T. garlic salt
1 T. crushed red pepper

2-3 T. chives
2 T. lemon juice
1 T. All Season salt

Mix and chill. Serve with carrot sticks, radishes, celery sticks, cauliflower, broccoli, etc.

Yield: about 3¼ cups

Shirley J. Todd
Needville, Texas

CHINESE OYSTER DIP

1 c. sour cream
¼ c. Oyster sauce

1 T. sugar
¼ t. Tabasco

Process and chill 1 to 2 hours. Serve with raw vegetables.

Yield: about 1¼ cups

Becky Karavatakis
Lafayette, La.

CURRY VEGETABLE DIP

1 c. mayonnaise
1 t. ginger, grated
1 clove garlic, minced
½ t. salt

2 T. chopped green onions
1 t. curry or more to taste
1 T. lemon juice or more to
taste

Put all ingredients in blender or processor, except lemon juice. Blend until smooth. Add lemon juice. Good with all types of raw vegetables.

Yield: 1 cup

Midge Scardina
Baton Rouge, La.

BLACK AND BLEU DIP

2 cans chopped ripe olives
3-oz. bleu cheese,
  crumbled
1 sm. onion, minced

Dash garlic powder
½ t. lemon juice
1 pt. sour cream
Dash white pepper

Combine and refrigerate. Serve cold with vegetables, or chips.

Yield: about 3 cups

Becky Karavatakis
Lafayette, La.

ASPARAGUS DIP

14-oz. can asparagus
  spears, drained
1 c. Creole cream cheese
½ t. lemon juice

¼ t. Tabasco sauce
¼ t. dill weed
Salt and pepper, to taste

Process or blend until smooth. Serve with raw vegetables.

Yield: about 2½ cups

Becky Karavatakis
Lafayette, La.

CUCUMBER DIP

3 cucumbers, peeled,
  seeded, and grated
½ med. onion, grated

8-oz. Philadelphia cream cheese
1 t. lemon juice
Salt to taste

Combine cucumbers, onion, and cheese. Add 1 teaspoon or more lemon juice. Salt to taste. Refrigerate until ready to serve. Serve with vegetables, crackers or chips.

Yield: about 3 cups

Alice Eastin
Lafayette, La.

LIGHT VEGETABLE DIP

8-oz. lo-cal bleu cheese dressing
8-oz. lo-cal cottage cheese
½ t. dry parsley flakes

Process or blend almost smooth. Serve with raw vegetables.

Variations: 1) try different lo-cal dressings; 2) substitute lo-cal yogurt for cottage cheese; 3) add 1 t. dry minced onions; 4) add 1 t. curry powder.

Yield: 1 pint

COTTAGE YOGURT DIP

1 c. cottage cheese
¼ c. yogurt
3 green onions w/tops

1 med. dill pickle, chopped
Dash Tabasco
Salt and pepper

Remove top from onions and slice thin. Reserve. Process cottage cheese, onion bottoms, yogurt and dill just until combined. Add Tabasco, salt and pepper, to taste. Spoon into serving bowl and garnish with green onion tops.

Yield: about 1¼ cup

Becky Karavatakis
Lafayette, La.

GINGER DIP

1 c. mayonnaise
1 c. sour cream
1 med. onion, grated
¼ c. fresh parsley,
   minced
5-oz. can water chestnuts
   minced

3 T. candied ginger,
   minced
1 sm. clove garlic, minced
1 T. soy sauce
2-3 dashes Tabasco sauce
¼ t. dill weed

Combine and chill. Serve as a dip for vegetables.

Variations: 1) Omit garlic and serve with fresh fruit; 2) As a spread, add 3 oz. pkg. Philadelphia cream cheese.

Yield: about 3 cups

Becky Karavatakis
Lafayette, La.

VEGETABLE DIP II

1 small glass Kraft Roka Blue Cheese
4 oz. Philadelphia cream cheese
1 T. "B.V. Beef Extract"
1 sm. onion, finely grated
1 pt. Hellmann's mayonnaise

Mix first 4 ingredients. Add mayonnaise; blend together. Serve with sticks of fresh, crisp raw carrots, celery, green peppers or your favorites.

Yield: 2⅔ pints

Vivian Mays
Lafayette, La.

ALMOND MARMALADE DIP

¼ c. orange juice
½ c. orange marmalade

8 oz. pkg. cream cheese
½ c. toasted almonds

Cream orange juice with cream cheese in processor or blender. Add marmalade and toasted almonds. Process until almonds are minced fine. Serve as a dip for fresh fruit.

Yield: 1 ¾ cups

Becky Karavatakis
Lafayette, La.

ORANGE YOGURT DIP

8-oz. orange yogurt
½ c. cranberry-orange relish

½ t. Fenugreek

Combine and use for dip with fresh fruit.

Yield: 1 ½ cups

Becky Karavatakis
Lafayette, La.

FRUIT DIPS

7-oz. jar marshmallow cream
8-oz. pkg. cream cheese
Dash or ginger

1 T. grated orange rind
4 T. concentrated orange
juice

Process or blend until smooth. Serve with fresh pieces of fruit.

Yield: 2 cups

Becky Bishop
Lafayette, La.

LEMON CREAM

4 lg. eggs
⅓ c. sugar
1 t. unflavored gelatin
2 T. cold water

2 T. lemon juice
1 t. fine grated lemon zest
½ c. sour cream
Sprig of mint

Sprinkle gelatin over water in small bowl. Reserve. Beat egg whites to soft peak. Add yellows and beat until well blended. Continue beating and slowly add sugar until egg mixture is about tripled. Heat gelatin mixture over low heat until dissolved. Remove from heat; stir in lemon and lemon zest. Stir egg mixture and sour cream into gelatin miture until well blended. Cover with wax paper and refrigerate. Just before serving, stir well and garnish with sprig of lemon.

Yield: about 2 cups.

CHOCOLATE COFFEE GLAZE

¼ c. strong coffee
¼ c. light corn syrup

⅓ c. butter
8 oz. semisweet chocolate,
crushed

Melt butter in sauce pan over medium heat. Stir in coffee and corn syrup until boiling; cook 30 seconds. Remove from heat. Stir in chocolate until smooth. let cool. Serve at room temperature.

Yield: about 1¼ cups

Becky Karavatakis
Lafayette, La.

Note: Both of these dips are excellent served surrounded with fresh strawberries with stems left on.

HOT DIPS

THE "OYSTER ROCKEFELLER DIP"

2 pts. fresh shucked sm. oysters
¼ lb. oleo for sauteeing oysters
¼ lb. butter
1 lg. bunch green onions
1 lg. bunch parsley
2 10-oz. pkg. frozen, chopped
   spinach, cooked and drained
1 T. celery salt
2 T. Worcestershire sauce

2 T. Tabasco
1 T. horseradish
1 t. basil
1 t. marjoram
3 T. anisette
1 c. Italian bread
crumbs
¾ t. anchovy paste

Saute oysters in oleo until edges curl. Set aside. Chop onions and parsley very fine and saute in butter. Add all other ingredients and put in chafing dish. Serve warm with Melba Toast points or unsalted crackers.

Note: This dish also makes an excellent vegetable casserole dish for a buffet dinner. Can be kept up to 48 hours under refrigeration. T.W.

Yield: 3 pints

*Trudy Williams
Houston, Texas*

CRAWFISH AU GRATIN

5 T. butter
1 c. green onion tops,
    finely chopped
4 T. flour
2 c. coffee cream
¾ c. Taylor Sauterne wine
3 lbs crawfish tails

½ t. salt
1 t. white pepper
3 8-oz. pkgs. Kraft
American cheese
8-oz. Kraft Swiss cheese
Several dashes Tabasco

Melt butter in skillet. Add green onion tops and saute until wilted. Add flour and stir few seconds. Add cream, wine, salt and pepper. heat, stirring constantly. DO NOT BOIL. Add cheeses and stir until melted. Add Tabasco and crawfish. Place in glass dish in oven at 400° F. until thoroughly heated, do not brown. Serve as casserole or from chafing dish with pastry cups.

Yield: about ½ gallon

Dot Smith
Lafayette, La.

CRAB AU GRATIN

½ c. onions, minced
2 ribs celery, minced
1 stick butter
2 T. flour
6-oz. cheddar cheese,
    grated

½ pt. half and half cream
2 lg. egg yolks
1 lb. fresh white crabmeat,
picked
1 t. white pepper
Salt to taste

Saute onions and celery in butter until soft. Stir in flour. Add milk. Remove from heat; add egg yolks, crabmeat, cheese, salt and pepper. Bake in casserole dish at 350° F. for 30 minutes. Serve warm with tart or puff shells for filling.

Yield: about 2½ pints

Becky Karavatakis
Lafayette, La.

JOHN'S CRAB DIP

1½ sticks oleo
2 stalks celery w/tops
  chopped fine
3 lbs. crabmeat or
  seven 6-oz. cans
½ t. garlic powder
10½ oz. can cream of
  mushroom soup
OPTIONAL: 1 t. Kitchen
  Bouquet

2 large onions,
  chopped fine
3 T. parsley, chopped
1 lg. can evaporated milk
2 lbs. Velveeta cheese
  cut into small cubes
½ t. powdered thyme
Salt and red pepper, to taste
Crushed bread crumbs, if needed

Melt oleo in large black iron pot. Add onions and celery. Cook with lid on pot on low fire about 20 to 30 minutes, stirring to prevent sticking. Add parsley, crabmeat, evaporated milk, Velveeta cheese, garlic powder, cream of mushroom soup, and thyme. OPTION: if tan dip is desired, add 1 teaspoon Kitchen Bouquet. Cook about 1 hour on low with lid on pot, stirring occasionally to prevent sticking. Add salt and red pepper, to taste. After cooking check for thickness, if thicker dip is desired stir in fine crushed bread crumbs. Cook about 15 minutes longer on low.

Yield: about 100 servings

John J. Daigre
Lafayette, La.

CRAB MORNAY

1½ c. lump crab meat,
  picked but lumpy
3 T. flour
1¼ c. Half & Half
½ c. Gruyere cheese, grated
Salt and pepper, to taste

1 T. lemon juice
4 T. unsalted butter
3 green onion tops,
  thin sliced
3 T. onion, minced
3 T. grated Parmesan

Saute minced onions in 1 tablespoon butter until soft; stir in onion tops, lemon juice, crab meat, and adjust seasoning to taste. Reserve. Make a light roux of the remaining butter and flour, about 3 minutes. Reserve. Scald the milk; beat into roux mixture over medium heat until boiling, stirring constantly until smooth; reduce to simmer. Add cream and cheese, stirring until cheese is melted. Sprinkle Parmesan on top. Bake at 350° F. for 30 minutes. Serve warm from chafing dish with Mini Tart Shells or crackers.

Yield: about 3 cups

Becky Karavatakis
Lafayette, La.

CRABMEAT DIP

1 lb. lump crabmeat
8 oz. cream cheese
1 stick butter
1 clove garlic, chopped
  very fine

1 sm. onion, chopped
  very fine
Red pepper
Black pepper
Salt

Season crabmeat with salt and peppers. Saute onion and garlic in butter. Melt cream cheese in onion mixture, stirring constantly so it doesn't burn. Stir in crabmeat.

Yield: about 3 cups

Valerie Gonzalez
Baton Rouge, La.

BAKED CRAB ALMONDINE

2 8-oz. pkg. cream cheese
1 lb. white crab, flaked
¼ c. dry white wine

3-4 dashes Tabasco
2 t. lemon juice
½ c. toasted almonds, sliced

Process cream cheese with wine, lemon and Tabasco until smooth. Fold in crabmeat and spread into greased casserole dish. Top with sliced almonds. Bake at 350° F. for 15 to 20 minutes or lightly golden on top. Serve warm with crackers.

Yield: about 1 quart

SPINACH AND CRAB DIP

1 10-oz. pkg. frozen chopped
  spinach
1 bunch green onion w/tops
  chopped fine
White pepper and salt to taste

4 T. butter
1 lb. fresh white
  crabmeat, flaked
⅓ c. grated Parmesan
  cheese

Cook and drain spinach. Saute green onions in butter. Mix remaining ingredients together and heat thoroughly. Serve warm from chafing dish with La Petite Puff Shells or Mini Tart Shells or toast points.

Variation: add ¼ c. breadcrumbs, blend together and fill mushroom caps. Place on baking sheet and run under broiler until hot.

Yield: about 2½ cups

Becky Karavatakis
Lafayette, La.

CHOWDER JARLSBERG

2 lb. shrimp 51-55/lb., deveined and halved
2 T. butter
2 c. fresh mushrooms,
   sliced
½ c. green onion tops,
   chopped
1 sm. clove garlic, minced
3 pts. Half and Half cream
2 c. Jarlsberg cheese,
   shredded

½ c. Jarlsberg cheese,
1 c. frozen green peas,
   cooked and drained
½ c. carrots, shredded
¼ fresh parsley,
   chopped
¼ t. oregano, crushed
6 doz. Mini Tart Shells,
   prebaked (p.59)
1 t. dill weed

Saute shrimp in butter until pink. Add mushrooms, onions and garlic. Cook until vegetables are tender. Add cream, 2 cups cheese, peas, carrots, parsley and oregano. Stir over medium heat until hot, Do Not Boil. Transfer to chafing dish. Garnish with ½ cup Jarlsberg cheese and dill weed. Serve with Mini Tart Shells for filling.

Yield: 2 quarts or
   enough for 60 tarts

Becky Karavatakis
Lafayette, La.

CURRIED SHRIMP

1 lg. onion, chopped
1 med. apple, chopped
1 clove garlic, minced
3 lb. shrimp 31-35/lb.
½ stick butter
2 T. cornstarch

1 can Rotel tomatoes and
green chilies, chopped
2 t. curry powder
Salt and pepper
1 T. lemon juice
1 T. mayonnaise

Saute onion, apple and garlic in butter until lightly browned. Stir in cornstarch and simmer about a minute. Add tomatoes and curry powder. Season to taste with salt and pepper. Simmer five minutes. Add mayonnaise and lemon juice. Chill at least 2 hours to set flavors. Serve in sauce, hot or cold, with melba toast rounds or cucumber slices.

Yield: about 100

Becky Karavatakis
Lafayette, La.

FISH PLAKI

½ c. olive oil
3 lg. fresh tomatoes, wedged
1 lg. onion, chopped
1 c. fresh parsley, chopped

1 clove garlic, minced
½ t. oregano or
Italian seasoning
2 lbs. fresh firm fish

Saute onions in oil for 5 minutes. Add garlic, parsley and oregano; simmer 5 minutes longer. Add tomatoes and cook over medium heat until tomatoes are soft. Remove from fire and add fish, cut into cubes, and enough water to cover. Return to fire and cook until fish is done. DO NOT STIR. Spoon into patty shells and serve warm.

Variations: Chicken Plaki — use 2 lbs. boned, cubed chicken or Beef Plaki — use 2 lbs. rib eye or filet, cubed.

Yield: about 5 dozen

Ted Karavatakis
Lafayette, La.

COCKTAIL MEATBALLS STROGANOFF

1½ lb. ground round
½ lb. ground lean pork
½ c. milk or cream
½ c. bread crumbs
2 lg. eggs, beaten
2 T. butter

½ t. ginger
½ t. allspice
1½ t. Tony's seasoning
2 med. onions, minced
Stroganoff Sauce

Saute onions in butter for 5 minutes or until clear. Combine with remaining ingredients in large bowl. Shape into 1" balls and bake 10 to 15 minutes or until lightly browned in 400° F. oven — or deep fry at 375° F. Freezes well for up to 4 weeks. Serve from chafing dish in Stroganoff Sauce.

Stroganoff Sauce:
1 lg. onion, minced fine
4 T. butter
4 T. flour
1½ c. beef broth

½ c. dry white wine
1 c. sour cream
½ t. dillweed
Salt and pepper, to taste

Saute onion in butter, until soft. Stir in flour until well blended. Stir in stock and wine and continue stirring until mixture thickens. Remove and stir in sour cream and dill weed. Season to taste with salt and pepper. This makes about 3½ cups.

Yield: 6 to 7 dozen

Becky Karavatakis
Lafayette, La.

MEATBALLS IN CREAM SAUCE

2 lg. eggs, beaten
½ c. bread crumbs
3¼ lbs. ground round
½ stick butter

1 med. onion, chopped
½ t. Tony's seasoning
½ t. salt

Mix together and form into 1″ balls. Deep fry until brown or bake until brown. Serve warm from chafing dish in Cream Sauce.

Cream Sauce
¼ c. butter
¼ c. flour
2 c. chicken broth
¼ t. pepper

¼ t. lemon pepper
¼ t. salt
2 t. dill weed
1 c. sour cream

Melt butter in saucepan; stir in flour. Stir in broth, salt, peppers, and dill weed. Stir while cooking over medium heat until thickened. Remove from heat and stir in sour cream.

Yield: 6 to 7 dozen

Sharron Brown Mayers
Baton Rouge, La.

POLYNESIAN CHICKEN NIBBLERS

1 lb. raw, boned, cubed
  chicken breasts
½ c. sugar

4 t. cornstarch
¼ c. tomato paste
1 c. water

Cut chicken to ¾″ cubes. Combine remaining ingredients and stir over medium heat until mixture boils. Continue cooking about one minute. Remove from heat; let cool. Pour over chicken; cover and refrigerate overnight. Bake at 325° F. for 40 to 45 minutes. Serve warm from chafing dish.

Yield: 4 to 5 dozen

Becky Karavatakis
Lafayette, La.

CHINESE MEAT BALLS WITH PEKING SAUCE

1½ lbs. lean ground round
6-oz. dark soy
4 cloves garlic, minced
2 T. rice vinegar

1 T. fresh ginger,
minced fine
2 T. sugar
Peking Sauce

Combine ingredients. Form into 1" balls. Place in baking pan and bake at 350° F. for 20 minutes. Cover with Peking Sauce and bake 10 minutes longer. Serve hot from chafing dish.

Peking Sauce
½ c. green onions w/tops
minced
2 cloves garlic, minced
¼ c. soy sauce

¼ c. water
1 t. fresh ginger, minced
1 T. honey
1½ T. rice vinegar

Combine. makes about ⅔ cup.

HOT CHILE DIP

1 med. red chile pepper, seeded
1 med. onion, wedged
2 cans Rotel diced tomatoes
and green chilies
1 lb. bag tortilla chips

1 T. sugar
1 t. salt
¼ t. ground oregano
2 dashes cumin
1 clove garlic

Process pepper, onion and garlic until chunky. Add remaining ingredients and process until blended, but not smooth. Warm tortilla chips in 200° F. oven for 10 minutes.

Yield: about 2¾ cups

Becky Karavatakis
Lafayette, La.

137

CHICKEN WITH PARSLEY SAUCE

*8 chicken breasts, boned
   and cubed about 1" each*
⅓ c. olive oil
1 clove garlic, quartered

1 t. salt
1½ c. water
Salt and pepper, to taste
Parsley Sauce

Saute garlic pieces in oil until browned. Discard garlic and cook the chicken pieces in oil until browned on all sides. Season with salt and pepper. Add water; cover, and cook until tender. Serve with Parsley Sauce.

Parsley Sauce
1 T. butter
2 T. flour
1 c. Half and Half cream
1 c. chicken stock

½ c. chopped parsley
Salt and pepper, to taste
2 lg. egg yolks
1 t. lemon juice

Heat butter and flour and blend well. Add cream and chicken stock, stirring until smooth and thickened. Add parsley, salt and pepper, and bring to a boil. Beat egg yolk, add lemon juice, and beat in a little of the hot sauce and gradually stir into remaining sauce. Stir over low heat until thickened, being careful not to boil after adding the eggs. Just before serving heat sauce and chicken; serve warm.

Yield: about 5 dozen

*Becky Karavatakis
Lafayette, La.*

BILL HANSEN'S CHILI

6 lb. chili meat
12 pods garlic, minced
2 lg. onions, cut in half
then sliced
Salt
Black and red pepper

3-oz. jar Mexene chili powder
4 15-oz. cans tomato sauce
4 cans Trappey's light red
kidney beans
6 jalapeno peppers, chopped,
more or less to taste

Break up meat with fork. Cover with salt, black pepper and some red pepper. Cook until brown; pour off water. Add onions and garlic. Simmer until tender. Add chili powder; mix well. Add tomato sauce, beans and 2 cans of water. Cook on low fire about 1 hour. Stir in jalapeno peppers.

Note: mash beans; blend and serve hot with chips. R.B.K.

Yield: about 2 gallons

Bill Hansen
New Orleans, La.

BACON AND COLBY DIP

½ lb. bacon, cooked
drained, and crumbled
2 c. colby cheese, grated
⅓ c. Half and Half cream
1 t. Worcestershire

¼ t. dry mustard
¼ t. onion or garlic
salt
¼ t. Tabasco or
to taste

Melt cream cheese in double boiler. Stir in colby until blended. Add remaining ingredients and mix well. Serve warm from chafing dish with melta toast rounds or slices of apples and pears that have been dipped in lemon juice.

Yield: about 3 cups

Becky Karavatakis
Lafayette, La.

PICADILLO

1 lb. lean ground beef
  or venison
¾ c. bell pepper, chopped
Dash black pepper
2 jalapenos, seeded and chopped
¾ c. onion, chopped
¾ c. almonds, slivered
3 tomatoes, peeled and chopped
1 6-oz. can tomato paste

2 lg. cloves garlic,
  minced
1 T. oregano
1 small jar pimentoes,
  chopped
¾ c. raisins
1 to 3 T. sugar
2 t. salt

Cover meat with water and boil for 30 minutes. Add remaining ingredients and cook over low heat for at least one hour. Serve in chafing dish with tortilla chips for dipping.

Yield: about 3½ pints

*Daryl Hause Tanner
Corpus Christi, Tx.*

TACO DIP

½ lb. lean ground beef
2 lb. Velveeta cheese, cubed
1 t. chili powder
1 med. onion, minced
2 T. butter

1 clove garlic, minced
1 10-oz. can Rotel diced
  tomatoes and green chilies
1 t. Tony's seasoning
Tabasco, optional

Saute onion and garlic in butter, about 5 minutes; reserve. Brown meat and drain. Place all ingredients in double boiler and heat until cheese is melted, stirring almost constantly or microwave on high in 4 qt. casserole dish for 8 minutes, turning every 2 minutes. Serve warm with a variety of Mexican style chips.

Yield: about 4½ cups

*Becky Karavatakis
Lafayette, La.*

PARTY BROCCOLI DIP

1 onion, chopped fine
1 stick butter
4 10-oz. pkg. chopped broccoli
1 can cream of mushroom soup
1 pt. sour cream
Lemon pepper to taste
Morton's Nature Seasonings to taste

1½ rolls garlic cheese
1 t. MSG
1 lg. can mushrooms,
drained, chopped fine
1 lg. jar pimento,
chopped

Saute onions in butter. Cook broccoli according to package directions; drain well. Melt cheese in mushroom soup; add sour cream, MSG, mushrooms, pimento, and onions. Combine broccoli and cheese mixture. Season to taste and heat through. Serve hot with bread sticks, crackers, etc.

Yield: about 3 pints

Kay Dillard
LaPlace, La.

MOCK OYSTER DIP

1 pkg. chopped frozen broccoli
1 lg. onion, minced
1 stick butter
6-oz. roll garlic cheese
Dash Tabasco

10.5-oz. can cream of
mushroom soup
8-oz. can mushroom stems
and pieces w/juice

Cook broccoli until all water is gone. Saute onion in butter; add soup, mushrooms and juice. Break up cheese and add to mixture. Add Tabasco and broccoli. Mix well. Serve warm from chafing dish with chips and crackers.

Yield: about 2½ pints

Alice Eastin
Lafayette, La.

BROCCOLI MORNAY

3 10-oz. pkg. chopped
  frozen broccoli
10½ oz. can cream of
  celery soup, undiluted
10½ oz. can cream of
  onion soup, undiluted

8 oz. Lorraine Swiss cheese
1 lg. onion, chopped fine
¼ c. grated Parmesan cheese
¼ t. garlic powder
2 T. butter
4 oz. American cheese

Steam broccoli and drain. Saute onion in butter 2 minutes on high in microwave or 5 minutes on stove. Process cheeses with seasonings. Mix together and refrigerate until half hour before serving. Heat over low fire and serve warm from chafing dish with crackers.

Yield: about 2 quarts

Becky Karavatakis
Lafayette, La.

HOT ARTICHOKE DIP

1 c. artichoke hearts,
  chopped
1 c. Parmesan cheese,
  grated
1 c. mayonnaise

½ t. garlic salt
½ c. green onions,
  chopped
½ t. white pepper
Paprika

Preheat oven to 350° F. Combine all ingredients, except paprika, and mix gently. Spead in 1½ quart baking dish; sprinkle with paprika and bake for 20 to 25 minutes. Serve warm with chips or raw vegetables.

Yield: about 2½ cups

John J. Daigre
Lafayette, La.

GNOCCHI VERDI

2 10-oz. pkg. frozen
  spinach, cooked, drained
8-oz. ricotta cheese
2-oz. piece Parmesan cheese
  hand grated
3 T. butter

1 ¼ c. flour
½ t. salt
⅛ t. pepper
⅛ t. powdered nutmeg
Boiling salted water

Chop spinach very fine. Stir in ricotta cheese and eggs. Add half of the cheese, ¼ cup of flour, salt, pepper, and nutmeg. Mix together well. Cover and refrigerate about 1 hour. Roll mixture by tablespoonful to football shape. Roll each in flour. Bring salted water to boil. Carefully slide rolls, 6 to 8 at a time into water; reduce heat to medium, and cook until slightly puffed and soft-firm to the touch, 3 to 4 minutes. Remove with slotted spoon and drain on paper towels. Bring water back to boil and add next batch, reduce heat and repeat procedure until all are cooked. Transfer in a single layer to greased baking pan. Melt butter and dribble over gnocchi. Sprinkle remaining cheese over top. Broil 2 to 3 minutes, until cheese is lightly browned. Serve hot.

Yield: about 4 dozen

Becky Karavatakis
Lafayette, La.

HOT MEXICAN BEAN DIP

3½ c. pinto beans
   drained and mashed
½ c. American cheese,
   shredded
1 t. garlic salt
2 t. vinegar

½ t. liquid smoke
1 t. chili powder
½ t. salt
Dash cayenne pepper
2 t. Worcestershire sauce
4 slices crisp bacon, crumbled

Reserve bacon. Combine remaining ingredients and heat. Stir in bacon bits. Serve hot or cold, with tortilla chips.

Yield: about 2 pints

Sharron B. Mayers
Baton Rouge, La.

RIO GRANDE DIP

1 can pinto beans, mashed
1 stick butter
4-oz. Monterrey Jack cheese
4 Jalapeno peppers, chopped fine

1 med. onion, minced fine
1 sm. clove garlic, crushed
¼ t. chili powder
1 T. chopped ripe olives

Combine all ingredients over medium heat and stir until cheese is melted. Refrigerate several hours. Serve warm with warm toasted tortilla chips.

Yield: about 3 cups

Becky Karavatakis
Lafayette, La.

CON QUESO DIP

2 lb. Velveeta cheese,
  cubed
16 oz. can Rotel tomatoes,
  drained and chopped
1 t. chili powder

4 oz. can whole green
  chilies, drained,
  chopped
Picante Sauce (p. 20)

Melt cheese in double boiler; stirring occasionally. Combine with tomatoes, chili powder and green chilies. Mix well. Adjust hotness with Picante Sauce.

Yield: 5 to 6 cups

Janice Ehni
Lafayette, La.

HOT CHEESE DIP

2 lbs. Velveeta cheese
2 med. onions, chopped

1 qt. Hellmann's mayonnaise
12 oz. jar jalapeno peppers

Let cheese come to room temperature. Remove seeds from peppers. Place onions and peppers in blender or processor and grate together. Heat cheese, mayonnaise, onions, and peppers on low heat until smooth. Serve with Doritos.

Note: Other mayonnaise may tend to make this very greasy. C.C.

Yield: about 2½ quarts

Carol Christie
Lafayette, La.

MUSHROOM DIP

¼ cup butter
1 med. onion, minced
1 clove garlic, minced
1 lb. mushrooms, sliced

½ t. white pepper
8 oz. sour cream
1-2 dashes Tabasco sauce

Saute onion and garlic in butter 5 minutes. Add mushrooms, pepper and Tabasco. Saute until mushrooms are tender. Fold in sour cream. Serve warm with zucchini slices or crackers.

Yield: about 3 cups

GARLIC AND POTATO DIP

6 cloves, garlic, minced fine
4 4″ red potatoes, mashes
½ c. olive oil
½ c. corn oil

¼ c. rice vinegar, plus
water to make ⅓ c.
Juice of one lemon
Salt and pepper to taste

Mash garlic into potatoes until well blended. Mix oils, lemon, vinegar and water together. Blend into potato mixture a little at a time until smooth. Heat over double boiler and serve warm with boiled shrimp for dipping.

Variations: for Anchovy and potato dip: omit garlic and add 1 t. anchovy paste and 1 T. grated onion.

Yield: 2¾ to 3 cups

Becky Karavatakis
Lafayette, La.

COLD HORS d'OEUVRES

SNOW PEA WREATH

½ lb. snow peas
2½ oz. crab meat,
    picked and flaked
1 t. horseradish
¼ t. red pepper

1 c. sour cream
2 scallion tops,
    minced
1 Wreath

Trim stems from peas. Lower peas into 1 quart boiling, salted water in fry basket. Reduce heat to medium and simmer 1 minute. Drain and dip in iced water. Drain and refrigerate at least half hour. Combine remaining ingredients and mix well. Put ½ mixture at a time into pastry bag with ¼" plain or fluted tip. Carefully slit one side of pea pod. Pipe filling into peas. Arrange with sides touching to hold upright. Chill at least one hour.

Variations: Substitute thin sliced pepperoni, minced or 1 small can deviled ham. R.B.K.

Wreath
1 8" styrofoam wreath
Fresh parsley

foil to cover
Bunch red grapes

Using a knife cut ½" wide wedges ½" deep, with center of wedges 1½" apart, all around the wreath. Cut foil into strips about 3" x 12" and wrap wreath completely, pressing foil into wedges. Place snow peas in wedges and snip parsley and slide between peas. Garnish with a scattering of grapes in groups of three around the wreath.

Yield: about 5 dozen

Becky Karavatakis
Lafayette, La.

LIGHT MUSHROOM STUFFED CELERY

½ c. mushrooms, minced
12 3″ long celery sticks
3 T. low-fat mayonnaise,
   or low-fat bleu cheese
   dressing

1 med. green pepper, seeded,
   minced
Optional: Tabasco to taste
12 cherry tomatoes
6 6-inch long green onions

Combine mushrooms, green peppers and mayonnaise. Add Tabasco if desired. Fill celery sticks. Arrange in wreath shape on a lettuce bed alternating with cherry tomatoes. Remove roots and trim tops of green onion to about 6″ in length. With paring knife split the tops in 4 to 5 places about 3″ down the stems. Place in ice water for 20 to 30 minutes to curl ends. Stand in center in small vase.

Yield: 1 dozen.

CURRIED YAM BALLS

5 lbs. La. Yams (sweet potatoes)
1 c. (2 med.) onions,
   minced
1 lg. bell pepper,
   minced
1 c. mayonnaise

½ c. chicken stock
2 T. curry powder
1 t. white pepper
⅓ c. fresh parsley
1 c. sour cream
Salt to taste

Remove skins from potatoes and scoop out using a 1″ melon baller. Boil potato balls in salted water until slightly firm. Drain and cool. Mix mayonnaise, sour cream, chicken stock and curry powder together. Adjust seasoning with salt and pepper to taste. Pour mixture over potatoes and mix gently to coat evenly. Snip parsley over top and refrigerate at least 2 hours to set the flavors. Serve cold.

Yield: about 7 dozen

Becky Karavatakis
Lafayette, La.

149

STUFFED ZUCCHINI

Med. zucchini (8-9")
3-oz. cream cheese
4-oz. Bleu cheese,
    crumbled

2 T. brandy
Dash ground nutmeg
8 pimento stuffed olives,
    sliced

Trim ends from zucchini. Pare lengthwise every other ¼". Cut in half crosswise. Use apple corer to remove seeds. Combine cheeses, brandy and nutmeg. Press cheese mixture into zucchini. Wrap in plastic wrap and chill at least one hour. Remove and slice about ¼" thick. Top with slice of olive (or small piece of pimento).

Yield: about 2½ dozen

POTATO TOES CAVIAR

16 2" new potatoes
1 c. sour cream
6 oz. caviar, red or black
1 t. Tony's seasoning

¼ c. minced onions
3 large hard-boiled eggs,
    chopped fine
1 t. chopped parsley

Boil potatoes in skins until tender; drain. Cut small slice of skin off bottom so potato will sit flat with cut half up. Scoop out center with melon baller. Blend or process scooped out portion of potatoes with sour cream, seasoning, onions, and boiled eggs. Fill potato toes with filling and top with caviar and sprinkle with parsley.

Variation: omit sour cream and caviar. Use only 1 boiled egg. Add 1 T. mustard, ¼ c. olive oil and 2 T. minced dill pickle. Top with anchovy rolled in caper. Garnish with a small sprig of parsley.

Yield: 16

Becky Karavatakis
Lafayette, La.

ARTICHOKE SQUARES

2 6-oz. jars marinated artichokes
1 med. onion, chopped
1 sm. clove garlic, minced
4 lg. eggs, beaten ·
6 square crackers, crushed
1½ t. dried parsley

Dash Tabasco
½ t. Italian seasoning
¼ t. salt
¼ t. pepper
2 c. cheddar cheese, grated

Drain juice from 1 jar artichokes to skillet. Saute onion and garlic in juice. Drain juice from other jar, discard. Chop artichokes and combine with all other ingredients. Press into 9″ x 13″ well greased baking pan. Heat oven to 325° F. and bake for 30 minutes. Cool 10 minutes. Cut into 1¼″ squares.

Yield: about 70

Marsha Runnels
Baton Rouge, La.

CAT EYES
CHUTNEY MARBLES

6-oz. bleu cheese,
   crumbled
8-oz. pecans, chopped fine

6-oz. Cranberry Chutney,
   (p.27) chopped fine
12-oz. cream cheese

Combine ingredients and form into 1″ balls. Chill.

Yield: about 4 dozen

Becky Karavatakis
Lafayette, La.

CHICKEN BALLS

4 t. white sesame seeds
1 lb. ground chicken
1 sm. onion, minced
¼ t. powdered ginger
4 t. peanut oil

2 t. soy sauce
2 t. rice vinegar
1 med. egg
2 t. sugar
Horseradish Mustard

Heat skillet to medium and stir sesame seeds until lightly golden, but not browned; reserve. Combine chicken, onion, ginger, sugar, soy sauce, vinegar and egg; mix well. Form into 1″ balls. Heat oil to med.-low, about 250-275° F., and saute-fry until browned. Sprinkle sesame seeds into dish, and roll hot chicken balls around to pick up seeds. Cool to room temperature and serve with Horseradish Mustard.

Horseradish Mustard:
1 c. Mustard
4 T. horseradish

Combine and chill at least one hour before serving. Keeps refrigerated up to two weeks. This makes 1 cup.

Yield: about 30

Becky Karavatakis
Lafayette, La.

CHICKEN PICO DE GALLO

3 whole chicken breasts
2 T. butter
1 sm. yellow onion, minced
8 lg. green chili peppers
2 yellow banana peppers
5 med. tomatoes

5 scallions with tops, chopped
¼ t. coriander
2 T. olive oil
1 t. white vinegar
Salt

Saute minced onion in butter for 5 minutes. Cut chicken breasts into ¾" cubes and add to onions. Cover and cook gently until done. Arrange peppers and tomatoes on baking sheet and broil 5" from heat, turning often, until skins begin to char. Place between layers of paper towels and allow to cool. Peel, seed, and chop peppers and tomatoes. Season to taste with salt. Add chicken cubes, stir and place in refrigerator, covered, at least 2 hours. Serve cold in sauce with picks.

Yield: 5 to 6 doz. pieces
about 2 cups sauce

LIGHT CHICKEN LEMONI

2 whole boned chicken
breasts
1 pt. pearl onions

1 T. lemon juice
1 T. dried parsley
8-oz. fresh mushrooms

Cut chicken to chunks about ¾' x 1½" and place in non stick pan sprayed lightly with Pam. Brown on both sides over medium-high heat. Reduce heat; drizzle with lemon, and sprinkle with parsley. Prepare onions. Cut mushrooms in half lengthwise. Add onions and mushrooms to chicken; cover and simmer 10 minutes. Serve on platter surrounded with twisted slices of lemon.

Yield: about 2½ pints

Becky Karavatakis
Lafayette, La.

SWEET 'N SOUR FLOUNDER

1 lb. filet flounder
2 T. rice vinegar
½ t. salt
2 dashes white pepper
¼ c. cornstarch
2½ t. cornstarch
¼ c. water
1½ T. cold water
⅓ c. chicken broth
¼ c. sugar
2 T. peanut oil

1 T. soy
1 T. ketchup
1 lg. egg
⅓ c. flour
4 c. peanut oil
¼ c. onion, minced fine
1 T. fresh gingerroot
pared, minced
1 med. clove garlic, minced
3 T. rice vinegar

Cut into pieces about ¾" x 1½". Combine 2 tablespoons rice vinegar, ¼ teaspoon salt and dash pepper. Mix 2½ teaspoons cornstarch and 1½ tablespoons cold water until smooth. Add stock, sugar, soy and ketchup; stir until sugar is dissolved. Reserve. Mix ¼ cup corn-starch and ¼ cup cold water. Beat in egg. Add flour, ¼ teaspoon salt and dash pepper. Heat peanut oil in wok in 350° F. Drain fish. Dip ½ fish in batter. Remove; place one piece at a time in wok. Fry 6 to 8 pieces at a time until golden. Drain on paper towels. Bring oil back to 350° F. before frying each batch. Place fish on serving dish. Clean wok. Heat 2 tablespoons oil until hot. Reduce heat to medium. Add onion, ginger, and garlic; stir fry 10 seconds. Stir in stock mixture and cook 1 minute. Stir in remaining vinegar; cook 10 seconds. Pour over fish. Serve warm.

Variations: 1) Substitute red fish, haddock or cod; 2) Substitute 2 T. sesame oil and add ¼ c. sesame seeds to batter.

Yield: about 3 dozen

Becky Karavatakis
Lafayette, La.

SHRIMP DIJON

1½ lbs. 41-45/lb. shrimp
 raw, peeled and deveined
½ c. rice vinegar
1 med. onion, minced
2 T. butter

2 sm. cloves garlic, minced
¼ t. red pepper
1 T. lemon juice
3 shallots, chopped
2 T. chives, minced

Place shrimp in large Zip-loc bag. Combine remainder of ingredients and pour over shrimp. Remove air and seal bag. Refrigerate at least 2 hours or overnight. Drain shrimp. Melt 2 tablespoons butter in skillet. Add shrimp and saute until pink. Let cool. Pile on platter lined with lettuce, around a dish of Dijon Sauce for dipping. Garnish by sprinkling 2 tablespoons minced chives over shrimp.

Dijon Sauce
2 T. butter
2 T. flour
½ c. Half and Half cream
½ c. chicken broth

Dash Tabasco
½ t. salt
1 T. lemon juice
2 T. Dijon mustard

Melt 2 tablespoon butter in skillet. Stir in flour until smooth. Slowly add chicken broth, then milk, stirring constantly. Stir in mustard, Tabasco, salt and lemon juice. Makes about 1⅓ cups.

Yield: 60 to 64

Becky Karavatakis
Lafayette, La.

BARBECUED SHRIMP

½ c. butter
1 T. soy sauce
2 bay leaves
¾ t. cayenne pepper
⅛ t. rosemary (optional)
⅛ t. oregano
2 lb. large (31-35/lb.)
   shrimp, peeled to last joint only

½ c. olive oil
Juice of 1 lemon
1 T. black pepper
½ t. paprika
⅛ t. thyme
1½ t. salt
1 loaf soft French bread,
   cut into 1" cubes

Combine all ingredients except shrimp and French bread cubes. Heat in baking dish. Stir until blended together. Add shrimp, stir until well coated with sauce. Bake at 350° F. for 30 minutes, stirring 2 or 3 times while cooking.

Note: Cube one loaf French bread; serve with picks for dipping into sauce. This makes 5 to 6 dozen bites.

Yield: 5 to 6 dozen

John J. Daigre
Lafayette, La.

MARINATED SHRIMP

6 lb. shrimp, peeled
   31-35/lb.)
¼ c. apple cider vinegar
½ c. ketchup
3 T. lemon juice

1 T. Worcestershire
2 c. vegetable oil
5 oz. jar horseradish
5 oz. jar hot Creole mustard
Salt and pepper, to taste

Put shrimp in pan. Combine remaining ingredients. Pour over shrimp; cover and refrigerate overnight. Serve in marinade.

Yield: about 200

Peggy Meaux
Lafayette, La.

CRAB FINGERS REMOULADE

¾ c. minced onions
4 oz. jar capers, drained
1 c. fresh parsley, chopped fine
1 T. Creole mustard
1 c. peanut oil

½ c. olive oil
½ t. salt
1 t. black pepper
¼ c. wine vinegar
6 doz. crab fingers

Reserve crab fingers. Combine remaining ingredients and blend well. Chill covered. Serve from a hollowed out cabbage in center of platter surrounded with crab fingers.

Yield: about 3 cups
6 dozen

MARINATED GULF SHRIMP

4 lb. white gulf shrimp,
   31-35/lb. cooked and peeled
2¼ oz. can anchovies,
   rolled in capers
4 lg. lemons, thin sliced
3 lg. onions, thin sliced

1 T. horseradish
2 c. olive oil
¾ c. red wine vinegar
¼ c. water
1 T. Italian seasoning
¼ t. garlic powder

Reserve shrimp in container. Combine remaining ingredients and pour over shrimp. Cover and chill at least 24 hours, turning or stirring twice. Drain and serve with picks.

Yield: 10 to 12 dozen

Becky Karavatakis
Lafayette, La.

HOT HORS d'OEUVRES

ARTICHOKE BALLS

1 can artichoke hearts,
  drained and mashed
1 lg. egg, lightly beaten
½ c. olive oil

1 c. Italian bread crumbs
¾ c. Italian cheese,
  grated
¼ t. garlic puree

Mix all ingredients well. Form into 1″ balls. Roll in additional bread crumbs. Bake on lightly greased baking sheet at 300° F. for 10 to 15 minutes.

Yield: 3 to 4 dozen

Midge Scardina
Baton Rouge, La.

STRAIGHT JACKETS

2 14-oz. cans artichoke hearts
1 lb. thin sliced bacon
Toothpicks

Preheat oven to 450° F. Cut artichoke hearts in half; cut bacon strips in half crosswise and wrap around artichoke hearts; secure with toothpicks. Place on baking sheet and bake 8 to 10 minutes or until bacon is crisp, turning once. Drain and serve warm.

Yield: about 3 dozen

Celia Pope
Baton Rouge, La.

FRIED TATER SKINS

6 russet potatoes,   Salt
     about 3" x 4"   Peanut oil for frying
Tony's seasoning

Scrub potatoes. Pare circles from outer edges about 1½" in diameter, leaving about ¼" potato with the skin. Reserve remainder of potato for other use. (You should get 6 pieces from each potato.) Deep fry at 375° F. until golden brown. Drain between paper towels. Sprinkle tops with salt or Tony's seasoning. Serve warm.

Variation: Try Louisiana Yams....yum!

Yield: about 3 dozen   *Becky Karavatakis*
                                                  Lafayette, La.

SPINACH BALLS

2 pkgs. frozen chopped   ¾ c. oleo, melted
     spinach   1 c. Parmesan, grated
2 c. herb seasoned   1 T. garlic salt
     Pepperidge Farm   ½ t. thyme
     Dressing Mix   1 t. accent (optional)
2 onions, chopped fine   Dash cayenne pepper
6 lg. eggs, beaten   ¾ c. oleo, melted

Mix well. Form into balls. Bake on ungreased cookie sheet at 350° F. for 15 minutes.

Yield: 4 to 6 dozen   *Marguerite Hillegeist*
                                                Cypress, Texas

FRIED ZUCCHINI FINGERS

3 sm. zucchini (about 6")
½ c. flour
3 lg. eggs, beaten
1 c. crushed cracker crumbs
Peanut Oil

Dash garlic powder
¼ t. dried oregano
½ t. salt
Black pepper
Hot Mustard

Cut zucchini into 4 sections about 1½" long. Cut lengthwise into quarters. Combine salt, pepper, garlic and oregano. Sprinkle over sticks. Beat eggs with 1 tablespoon of water. Put flour and cracker crumbs in separate Zip-Loc bags. Place 6 zucchini sticks in flour and shake. Dip into egg mixture and then into cracker crumbs, covering completely. Transfer to cake rack and repeat procedure until all are finished. Heat peanut oil to 350° F. and cook until golden brown. Drain; serve warm with Hot Mustard.

Yield: about 4 dozen

ROQUEFORT SPROUTS

10-oz. Brussels sprouts
8-oz. Creole cream cheese
2-oz. Roquefort cheese
30 Mini Tart Shells (p.59)

¼ c. rice vinegar
½ t. lemon juice
1 T. Parmesan cheese

Steam Brussels sprouts. Split in half. Process cheeses with vinegar and lemon juice. Spoon into shells. Place ½ Brussels sprouts curved side up on top of mixture. Sprinkle with Parmesan cheese. Bake in 350° F. oven for 12 to 15 minutes. Serve warm.

Yield: about 30

Becky Karavatakis
Lafayette, La.

EGGPLANT PUFFS

1 med. eggplant, boiled whole   ½ t. garlic powder
½ c. Swiss cheese,   ½ t. lemon juice
  grated   ¼ c. bread crumbs
1 lg. egg, beaten   ½ t. salt
½ c. flour   ¼ t. pepper
Peanut oil for frying   Savory Sauce

Reserve flour and oil. Combine eggplant, egg, lemon juice, bread crumbs, salt and pepper in processor until blended. Shape into 1″ balls and refrigerate 1 hour. Dust in flour and deep fry at 375° F. until golden brown. Refrigerate or freeze. Serve warm with Savory Sauce.

Savory Sauce
1 sm. head garlic, minced   3 bay leaves
2 c. olive oil   ½ t. salt
1 c. rice vinegar   ½ t. white pepper

Cook garlic in olive oil until lightly browned. Add vinegar and bay leaves. Simmer for 5 minutes. Remove bay leaves. Makes 2½ to 3 cups.

Yield: about 4 dozen   Becky Karavatakis
                                                    Lafayette, La.

TEMPURA PEARLS

1 pt. pearl onions
1 c. flour
2 T. sesame oil

1 c. ice water
1 lg. egg yolk
3 c. peanut oil

Whisk egg; add ice water and stir. Whisk in flour. Dip onions in batter to cover. Heat oils to 375° F. in wok. Fry 6 to 8 at a time; remove with slotted spoon and drain on paper towel. Reheat oil before addition of each batch. Serve hot on picks plain or with dipping sauces.

Variations: 1) try mushroom caps; 2) use melon baller and cut turnips, carrots, or potatoes, yams, or beets.

Yield: 4 to 5 dozen

Becky Karavatakis
Lafayette, La.

OLIVE BALLS

1 lb. sharp cheese, grated
1 c. flour
¼ t. garlic salt
1 t. Worcestershire

1 lg. jar med. size
stuffed olives
⅓ t. red pepper

Coarsely grate cheese. Let stand at room temperature until consistency of soft butter. Combine flour, red pepper, and garlic salt. Mix well. Work cheese into flour making a dough. Add Worcestershire. Adjust seasoning to taste — should be peppery. Pat out about 1 teaspoon of mixture and form around the stuffed olive. Bake on well greased cookie sheet for 10 minutes at 400° F. Serve hot.

Yield: 7-8 dozen

Kim Bergeron
Lafayette, La.

SURPRISE OLIVE CHEESE PUFFS

1 c. cheddar cheese, shredded
¼ c. butter, softened
½ c. all purpose flour

½ t. paprika
¼ t. salt
24 small pimento stuffed olives

In a small bowl, with fork, blend cheese and butter. Stir in flour, paprika and salt. Mix well. Blot olives with paper towels. Divide dough into 24 pieces; mold a piece of dough around each olive. Arrange on cookie sheet and freeze until solid. Pack in plastic bags. About 20 minutes before serving, preheat oven to 425° F. Bake frozen cheese balls on cookie sheet 15-20 minutes or until lightly browned. Freezes well up to 2 months.

Yield: about 2 dozen

Susan Harrison
Lafayette, La.

MONTEREY BOMBS
STUFFED CHEESE BALLS

½ lb. Monterey Jack cheese w/
jalapeno peppers
¼ t. onion powder

½ c. flour
2 6-oz. jars Spanish olives stuffed w/ jalapeno peppers

Grate cheese. Mix flour and onion powder in processor. Add cheese and mix to make a ball. Take about a teaspoon of dough and form around olive. Place on greased cookie sheet and bake at 400° F. for 8 to 10 minutes. Serve warm.

Yield: 3 to 4 dozen

George Karavatakis
Lafayette, La.

FRIED CHEESE CUBES

1 10-oz. pkg. Cracker Barrel
  sharp cheddar cheese
2 lg. eggs, beaten w/
1 T. milk

¾ fine cracker crumbs
1 T. sesame seeds
1 T. sesame oil
3 c. peanut oil

Cut cheese into ¾" cubes. Dip in egg mixture; coat with cracker crumbs and sesame seeds. Heat oil in wok to 350° F. Fry 6 to 8 at a time 1 to 2 minutes until lightly browned. Drain on paper towels. Serve warm with Picante Sauce or Hot Mustard for dipping.

Variations: 1) any of the Cracker Barrel cheeses work well; 2) if different flavors are desired, add to egg mixture: garlic, onion, Tony's seasonings, etc.

Yield: 2 dozen

FRIED CHEESE

3 lb. loaf Mozzarella
2 c. flour
6 lg. eggs, beaten
3 t. water

4 c. bread crumbs
1 t. salt
3 c. olive or peanut oil

Cut into finger size portions, about 2" long by ¾" square. Put flour into plastic bag. Shake the cheese to coat. Beat eggs with water and salt. Dip cheese and roll in bread crumbs. Place on cookie sheet and freeze at least ½ hour. Heat oil to 375° F. and fry a few at a time, removing as soon as they turn golden brown. Serve warm.

Yield: 45

Becky Karavatakis
Lafayette, La.

CHEESE CUBES

1 loaf soft French bread
  with crust removed
1 stick butter
1 lb. sharp cheddar, grated
2 t. dried dill weed
2 lg. eggs, beaten

1 t. Worcestershire sauce
1 T. onion, grated
1 t. Parmesan cheese, grated
1 T. parsley
½ red pepper, crushed

Cut bread into 1" cubes. Reserve. Melt butter over medium heat. Stir in cheeses, dill weed, Worcestershire, onion, parsley and pepper until melted. Remove from heat and beat in eggs. Dip bread cubes in cheese mixture, coating top and sides completely. Place on cookie sheet lined with wax paper. Freeze. Pre-heat oven to 350° F. Bake frozen cubes 12 to 15 minutes. Serve hot.

Yield: about 5 dozen

SAUSAGE PECANS

16 oz. Hot bulk sausage
1 lb. Colby cheese, grated
½ t. Italian seasoning
1½ flour
½ c. whole wheat flour

4 t. baking powder
¼ t. cream of tarter
1 t. salt
1 t. sugar
1 c. pecan meal

Mix all ingredients together except pecan meal. Process to form a ball. Form into pecan shapes using 1 teaspoonful of mixture and roll in pecan meal. Freeze in airtight container. Bake at 350° F. 18 to 20 minutes.

Yield: 8 to 9 dozen

Becky Karavatakis
Lafayette, La.

PETE'S BACON WRAPS
ANTI-RUMAKI

1 lb. little smokie sausages
1 lb. sm. won ton wraps

1 lb. sliced bacon
Toothpicks

Cut bacon into 3 sections crosswise. Place one sausage diagonally across each won ton wrap. Fold wrap over ends of sausage and roll up. Wrap ⅓ slice of bacon around each and secure with a toothpick. Deep fry at 375° F. until golden brown. Serve warm with Hot Mustard or Sweet 'n Sour Sauce.

Yield: about 48

*Pete Karavatakis
Lafayette, La.*

HAWAIIAN RUMAKI

1 lb. boiled ham
1 lb. bacon, halved
¼ c. pineapple juice

2 oz. sliced Swiss cheese
1 sm. jar red cherries
¼ c. brown sugar

Cut ham into about 32 equal pieces. Place in zip-lock bag with pineapple juice and marinate several hours or overnight. Drain. Divide swiss cheese into 32 equal pieces. Top each ham piece with ½ cherry an a slice of cheese. Wrap with bacon and secure with toothpick. Roll in brown sugar. Broil until bacon is crisp.

Yield: 32

*Becky Karavatakis
Lafayette, La.*

ORIENTAL HAM BALLS

1 lb. ground lean ham
1½ lb. lean ground pork
2 c. bread crumbs
2 lg. eggs, beaten
1 c. Half and Half cream

2¼ c. brown sugar
¾ c. rice vinegar
½ c. water
1½ t. dry mustard

Combine ham, pork, bread, eggs and milk. Shape into 1" balls. Lightly coat inside of 2 quart casserole dish with oil. Place meatballs in casserole one layer deep. Combine the remaining ingredients and pour over meatballs. Bake at 325° F. for about 1 hour or until done.

Yield: about 8 dozen

HUNGARIAN HAM ROUNDS

½ stick butter
¼ c. Italian bread crumbs
¼ c. Swiss cheese, grated
1¾ c. minced ham

1 t. caraway seeds
1 c. sour cream
6 lg. eggs, beaten

Mix well. Drop by teaspoonful into greased mini-muffin tins. Bake at 375° F. for 15 to 18 minutes. Serve warm.

Yield: about 3 dozen

Becky Karavatakis
Lafayette, La.

ORIENTAL MEATBALLS

1 lb. ground round	1 clove garlic, minced
¼ c. light soy	2 T. water
1½ t. powdered ginger	2 T. sesame oil

Kneed sesame oil into ground round. Mix in other ingredients. Shape into small balls about 1″ in diameter. Bake at 375° F. for 15 to 20 minutes in baking pan. Drain on paper towels. Serve warm with Sweet and Sour Sauce or Hot Mustard.

Yield: about 3 dozen

CORNED BEEF SPHERES

2 12-oz. cans corned beef	1 t. Tony's seasoning
1 lg. onion, minced	1 c. Half and Half cream
1 T. parsley, minced	1 12½-oz. jar sauer-
½ c. butter, melted	kraut, drained
1 c. flour	2 lg. eggs, beaten
1 t. dry mustard	¼ c. water
1 c. Italian bread crumbs	Peanut oil for frying

Flake corned beef; saute with onion and parsley in butter for about 5 minutes. Stir in flour, mustard and Tony's. Continue stirring and slowly add milk, cooking until thickened. Remove from heat and stir in sauerkraut. Chill about 1 hour. Form into 1″ balls. Beat eggs with water. Dip each in egg and roll in bread crumbs. Refrigerate for about 1 hour longer or freeze until ready to use. Deep fry in oil at about 375° F. for 3 to 4 minutes or until golden brown. Serve warm with Hot Mustard.

Yield: about 3½ dozen

Becky Karavatakis
Lafayette, La.

SESAME CHICKEN

2 T. sesame seeds
1 lb. chicken, ground
2 scallions, minced
½ t. Fenugreek
2 t. sugar

2 t. soy
2 t. rice vinegar
1 sm. egg, beaten
2 t. sesame oil

Toast sesame seeds over medium heat for 2 minutes. Reserve. Combine chicken, scallions, Fenugreek, sugar, soy, vinegar and egg. Mix well. Roll mixture by tablespoonful. Roll in sesame seeds. Heat 1 teaspoon oil to medium heat. Place half balls in wok. Shake pan gently to roll balls around and cook until brown, about 3 to 5 minutes. Repeat with other half. NOTE: If making ahead. Reserve sesame seeds and freeze before frying. Freeze on cookie sheet. When firm, transfer to freezer-proof container. Serve warm, with or without sauce.

Yield: about 30

CHICKEN SPHERES

1 lb. raw, boned, diced chicken
¼ c. minced onions
¼ c. fine chopped cashews
¼ c. fine chopped mushroom

2 T. corn starch
2 T. soy sauce
1 T. white wine
2 lg. egg whites,
   stiffly beaten

Combine ingredients and process lightly. Roll into 1" balls. Fry at 375° F. until floating and golden. Serve warm.

Yield: 4 dozen

Becky Karavatakis
Lafayette, La.

CHICKEN RUMAKI

1 lb. chicken livers, divided
1 can water chestnuts
Toothpicks

1 lb. bacon, halved
¼ c. dry white wine

Marinate liver in white wine 1-2 hours. Top liver pieces with water chestnuts and wrap with bacon. Broil until bacon is crisp, turning once. Serve hot.

Yield: about 32

CHINESE NUGGETS

2 whole chicken breasts,
  boned and cubed 1"
1 lg. egg, beaten
⅓ c. water

2 t. sesame seeds
½ t. salt
2 c. peanut or sesame oil
½ c. flour

Beat egg with water. Add flour, sesame seeds, and salt. Stir until smooth. Heat oil to 375° F. Dip chunks in batter and fry four or five at a time until done, about 5 minutes. Serve with Hot Mustard or Sweet and Sour Sauce.

Yield: 40 to 50

Becky Karavatakis
Lafayette, La.

SOUVLAKIA

Leg of lamb or pork loin
Juice of 2 lemons
Oregano

1½ c. olive oil
1-2 bay leaves
Salt and pepper

Cut meat into 1'' cubes. Sprinkle seasonings over meat. Combine oil and lemon. Pour oil and lemon mixture over meat; add bay leaf. Marinate overnight, mixing once or twice. Skewer meat and cook over charcoal, basting and turning ¼ turn at a time until desired doneness.

Yield: about 3 dozen
6 dozen half size

Nick Karavatakis
Mantamados, Greece

FISH KABOBS

Juice of one lemon
Juice of one lime
¼ c. olive oil
2 lbs. cod steaks,
  cut 1'' thick
2 red bell peppers,
  cut into 1'' x 1'' pieces

1 t. salt
¼ t. white pepper
1 clove garlic, minced
1 t. dry basil leaves
1 t. dry oregano leaves
1 lg. orange cut into chunks,
  cut into 1'' x 1'' pieces

Combine lemon and lime juices. Beat in oil, garlic, basil, oregano, salt and pepper. Cut fish into 1'' cubes. Place fish in large Zip-loc freezer bag. Pour marinade over fish; remove air from bag and seal. Refrigerate 2 hours. Drain; reserve marinade. Pat fish dry. Skewer fish, bell pepper, orange, fish, orange, bell pepper, and fish. Broil 4 to 5 inches from heat, turning a quarter turn at a time and basting with reserved marinade at each turn. Heat remaining marinade and serve warm as a dipping sauce.

Yield: 18 to 20

Becky Karavatakis
Lafayette, La.

PUFF 'N STUFF BALLS

1 lb. cooked crabmeat,
  flaked
¼ c. celery, minced
¼ c. onion, minced
¼ c. carrots, grated
2 eggs, separated
¾ c. beer

¾ c. flour
½ t. paprika
½ t. white pepper
1 t. salt
1 T. oil
¼ t. paprika
Oil for frying

Combine crab with minced vegetables, ½ teaspoon pepper, and ¼ teaspoon paprika. Shape into small balls. Cover and refrigerate. Combine flour, white pepper, paprika, salt. Add egg yolks, beer, and oil. Whisk until smooth. Cover and refrigerate at least 2 hours or overnight. Beat egg whites until stiff peaks form. Stir batter and fold in egg whites. Using 2 forks, carefully roll crab rolls in batter. Fry in deep hot fat (350° F.) until brown, about 2 minutes. Drain on paper towels.

Note: Shrimp, crab claws, fish pieces or vegetables may be dipped in batter and fried to serve with crab balls.

Yield: 2 to 3 dozen

Marguerite Hillegeist
Cypress, Texas

BAYOU CRAB BALLS

1 lb. fresh white crab meat	2 t. lemon rind, grated
2 lg. eggs, boiled and	⅛ t. white pepper
chopped fine	½ t. salt
2 green onions w/tops	1 lg. egg, beaten
chopped fine	2 T. whipping cream
2 T. fresh parsley,	2 T. Worcestershire
chopped fine	½ t. Tabasco

Flake crab meat and combine with all other ingredients. Refrigerate 2 hours or place in freezer for ½ hour. Roll into balls about 1 to 1¼ inch in diameter. Roll balls in flour and deep fry at 375° F. until golden. Drain on paper towels and serve warm.

Yield: 3 to 4 dozen

ORIENTAL CRAB BALLS

1 lb. lean ground pork	1 t. sugar
½ lb. white crab meat	1 t. white pepper
4 oz. fresh mushrooms,	1 c. cornstarch
chopped fine	2 lg. eggs, beaten
1 can water chestnuts,	2 t. water
chopped fine	2 t. salt

Combine pork, crab, mushrooms, chestnuts, salt, sugar and pepper. Mix until well blended. Form into balls bout 1″ to 1¼″ in diameter. Beat egg with water. Roll balls in cornstarch to coat and dip into egg mixture. Heat 2″ oil in wok to 375° F. and fry until golden brown. Drain on paper towel and serve warm.

Yield: 4 to 5 dozen

Becky Karavatakis
Lafayette, La.

BACON CRAB BALLS

½ c. V-8 juice
1 lg. egg, beaten
1 c. dry bread crumbs
8 oz. fresh white crab
   meat, flaked

½ t. parsley, chopped
½ t. celery, minced
½ t. salt
Dash white pepper
1 lb. bacon strips, halved

Beat egg with V-8 juice. Add bread crumbs, seasoning, parsley, celery, and blend well. Add crabmeat and mix lightly, but thoroughly. Form into finger shapes with rounded teaspoon of mixture per roll. Wrap each one with ½ strip of bacon and secure with toothpick. Broil, turning to brown on both sides. Serve warm.

Yield: 32

ARTICHOKE SHRIMP RUMAKI

1 lb. shrimp, peeled
   (31-35/lb)
1 lb. bacon, halved

4 oz. Creole mustard
2 cans artichokes, halved
8 oz. Italian dressing

Mix mustard with dressing. Combine artichokes and shrimp; pour dressing mixture over, cover and refrigerate overnight. Place a shrimp on each artichoke half. Wrap bacon around and secure with toothpick. Broil until bacon is crisp, turning once.

Yield: about 32

Becky Karavatakis
Lafayette, La.

HOT MARINATED SHRIMP

2 lbs. shrimp, 46/50 count,
   peeled and deveined
⅓ c. olive oil
⅓ c. white rice vinegar
2 T. water

½ t. salt
½ t. white pepper
¼ c. parsley, chopped
3 T. lemon juice
2 cloves garlic, pressed

Saute shrimp in oil. Add vinegar, garlic, salt and pepper. Simmer until liquid is absorbed. Sprinkle with parsley and lemon juice, stir gently to mix. Serve warm.

Variation: use ¼ c. olive oil and sesame seed oil for the remainder of the ⅓ c. oil. Add 2-3 dashes soy sauce and reduce salt to ¼ t.

Yield: about 8 dozen

SHRIMP IN VESTS

1 lb. shrimp, 31-35/lb.
1 c. olive oil
1 lb. thin sliced bacon
2 cloves garlic, minced

2 T. dill weed
Juice of 2 lemons
1 t. oregano
Tabasco to taste

Combine oil, garlic, dill, lemon and oregano. Pour over shrimp; cover and refrigerate overnight. Cut bacon in half cross wise and wrap one piece around each shrimp. Secure with toothpick. Broil, turning once. Watch carefully as this dish is cooked in 5-6 minutes. Serve at once or store in refrigerator and reheat in oven at 375 ° F. 3-5 minutes or until warm.

Yield: about 32

Becky Karavatakis
Lafayette, La.

GRILLED SHRIMP

3 lb. shrimp, 41-45/lb.
1 lg. onion, chopped
1 c. olive oil
½ c. liquid crab boil
3 lb. sliced bacon

1 clove garlic, chopped
1 t. lemon juice
1 T. Worcestershire sauce
Dash Tabasco

Peel shrimp, leaving the tail to the first joint. Cut bacon crosswise into thirds. Wrap one slice bacon around each shrimp; secure with pick. Reserve. Saute onion, and garlic in 2 tablespoons olive oil until wilted. Add remaining oil, crab boil, lemon juice, Worcestershire, and Tabasco. Heat to boil and remove from heat. Cool 5 minutes. Pour over shrimp; cover and refrigerate 1 to 2 hours. Drain, reserving marinade for basting. Grill, turning often until bacon is crisp. Baste several times to keep shrimp from drying out. Serve warm.

Yield: about 10 dozen

SHRIMP RUMAKI

1 lb. shrimp 31/35 count
1 can sliced water chestnuts

1 lb. bacon, halved
¼ c. chili sauce

Marinate shrimp in chili sauce several hours or overnight. Top with water chestnut and wrap with bacon. Secure with toothpick. Broil until bacon is crisp, turning once. Serve hot.

Variations: 1) Omit chili sauce. Add dash of ginger to ¼ cup soy sauce and 1 teaspoon sesame oil; 2) Omit chili sauce. Marinate in 1 c. olive oil, mixed with 2 T. lemon juice, 1 t. oregano and 2 cloves minced garlic.

Yield: about 32

Becky Karavatakis
Lafayette, La.

SHRIMP COCONUTS

1 lb. shrimp, peeled and
  deveined
2 lg. eggs, lighten beaten
¼ c. grated coconut or
2 T. cream de coconut

1 t. coriander
1 T. cornstarch
½ t. salt
3 c. peanut oil

Combine all ingredients in processor and process off and on until
shrimp is minced and ingredients are well blended. Place in covered
dish and freeze 20 minutes to chill well. Heat oil in wok to 375° F.
Roll mixture by level tablespoon to shape like coconuts. Fry about 6
at a time until golden; drain on paper towels. Return heat to 375° F.
before each addition. Serve warm.

Yield: 2½ to 3 dozen

SALMON-TOFU SPHERES

1 lg. can red salmon
¼ c. soy sauce
½ t. rice vinegar
½ t. salt
10 oz. tofu

½ t. sugar
2½ T. flour
2 t. grated ginger
⅓ c. flour
Peanut oil for frying

Heat salmon to boil with soy and vinegar; remove to cool. Drain;
remove all skin and bones. Flake; cut tofu into about 6 to 8 equal
pieces. Place in sauce pan with 3 cups of water and boil over medium
heat 2 minutes; drain in cloth lined sieve. Combine salmon, tofu, 2½
tablespoon flour, sugar and salt. Shape into 1" balls. Lightly roll each
ball in flour. Heat oil in wok or fryer to 325° F. Fry until golden
brown. Drain on paper towels. Place ¼ c. soy in bowl; add grated
ginger in center. Do not stir.

Yield: about 36

Becky Karavatakis
Lafayette, La.

PORK LOBSTER SPIRALS

1 lb. lean ground pork
4 oz. lobster tail, minced
½ c. water chestnuts,
   chopped
2 green onions w/tops,
   chopped fine
1 recipe Cream Cheese Pastry (p.60)

½ t. ground ginger
2 T. light soy
1 clove garlic,
   minced
¼ c. unsalted top crackers,
   finely crushed

Cook pork over medium heat until done, but not dry. Combine other ingredients. Divide pastry into 4 equal pieces. Roll each to about 9x12. Divide filling into 4 portions. Spread each on pastry across long side. Roll like jelly roll and seal edge with a little water. Place seam side down on ungreased baking sheet. Bake at 375° F. for 30 to 35 minutes. Cool 10 minutes and slice into 1" wide slices. Serve warm.

Yield: 3 to 4 dozen

Becky Karavatakis
Lafayette, La.

TUNA TEASERS

1 c. flour
1½ t. baking powder
1 t. onion salt
½ t. curry powder
Dash cayenne

¼ c. oleo
½ c. milk
1 6½-oz. can tuna
1 c. grated sharp cheese
1 T. chopped green pepper

Combine first 5 ingredients. Cut in oleo. Add milk, stir. Add remaining ingredients. Drop by teaspoonful on greased cookie sheet. Bake at 450° F. for 10-15 minutes.

Variation: Substitute ½ lb. fresh minced shrimp or crawfish. Add ½ t. Tony's seasoning, and top with a thin slice of almond. R.B.K.

Yield: 42

Mildred Moench Tuten
Ruston, La.

CRAWFISH TAMALES

1 lb. cleaned crawfish tails,
    ground
1 lg. onion, minced
1 rib celery, minced
1 clove garlic, minced
2 T. butter
1 t. salt

1½ to 2 T. Tabasco
1 t. salt
1 lb. corn meal
⅔ c. Crisco
1 T. tomato paste
1 pkg. corn husks
½ c. chicken or beef broth

Wash husks and trim to about 5" on cross grain x 2½" long. Soak overnight in water. Next day, heat Crisco in cast iron skillet; stir in corn meal and teaspoon salt. Stir until golden in color. Add enough broth to make a thick paste. Remove from heat; cool. Reserve. Saute onion, celery, and garlic in butter until soft. Stir in crawfish, teaspoon salt, Tabasco and tomato paste. Simmer over low heat about 10 minutes. Remove from heat and let cool. Spread a layer of corn mixture about ⅛ thick, the length of the husk, from one end across about half the width. Put a strip of crawfish mixture down center of the corn mixture and roll up. (This can be done thru a pastry bag.) Refrigerate until ready to serve. Heat just before serving. (Can be heated in rice cooker.) Serve warm.

Variations: 1) ground shrimp; 2) 1¼ lb. lean, browned, ground beef, drained.

Yield: 6 to 7 dozen

Becky Karavatakis
Lafayette, La.

CRAWFISH BOUDIN

2 lb. peeled crawfish tails
1 c. yellow onions, chopped
2 scallions w/tops, chopped
8 peppercorns
3 whole cloves
1 t. salt
1 bay leaf, broken
1½ c. yellow onions,
   chopped
1 Jalapeno pepper, seeded,
   chopped
3 scallions w/tops, chopped

1 T. salt
2 lg. cloves garlic, minced
¼ t. basil
3 c. cooked rice
1 t. ground Fenugreek
   or allspice
1 t. cayenne pepper
1 t. black pepper
1 c. parsley, chopped
1 dried red chili pepper,
   crumbled
1½ c. dry bread crumbs

Heat 1 cup onions, 2 scallions, peppercorns, cloves, bay leaf and 1 teaspoon salt in 1 quart water. Add crawfish and bring to boil. Reduce heat and simmer 3 minutes. Drain. Combine crawfish mixture with 1½ cups onions, Jalapeno pepper, and 3 scallions. Grind together. Reserve bread crumbs. Return to bowl and knead in remaining ingredients. Form ball with about 1 tablespoonful mixture. Roll in finely ground dry bread crumbs. May be frozen at this point. Heat oil to 375° F. and fry for 3 to 4 minutes or bake at 375° F. for 10 to 12 minutes. Serve warm.

Variation: Use 1½ lb. trimmed pork, cut into 1½" chunks. Reduce heat and simmer 1½ hours. Yield: 9 to 10 dozen. R.B.K.

Yield: 10 to 12 dozen

Becky Karavatakis
Lafayette, La.

THREE LITTLE PIGS

⅔ lb. Little Smokies
about 32

1 batch biscuit dough
8 slices Velveeta cheese

Roll dough on floured board. ⅛" thick. Cut with 2" cutter. Cut each slice cheese into 4 squares. Put one square in center of each biscuit. Place one sausage across each and roll up. Place on lightly greased baking sheet with seam side down. Bake in preheated oven at 425° F. for 6 to 8 minutes, or until golden brown. Serve warm.

Yield: about 32

Trudy Karavatakis
Lafayette, La.

BEEF QUICHE

1 unbaked pie shell (10")
1 lb. lean ground beef
Salt and pepper to taste
¼ c. onion, chopped
¼ c. green pepper, chopped
¼ c. green onion tops, minced
¼ c. parsley, chopped
1 T. cornstarch
2 or more T. Worcestershire

1 T. cornstarch
½ c. mayonnaise
1½ c. grated cheese
½ c. milk
2 lg. eggs
Dash lemon juice,
optional
Chopped pimento,
optional

Brown meat and drain excess fat. Saute onions in meat. Add other ingredients and mix. Place in unbaked pie shell and bake at 350° F. for 45 minutes.

Note: for mini size, use 36 unbaked Mini Tart Shells. Mince all ingredients or chop fine. Spoon into shells and bake at 350° F. for about 15 minutes. R.B.K.

Yield: 1 10" pie or
about 36 mini tarts

Eva Dell Daigre
Lafayette, La.

KIBBI

1 lb. Bulgur wheat	*1 lb. Kibbi meat*
1 lb. ground round	*2 lg. onions, chopped*
1 t. all spice	*½ t. dried mint*
1 t. cinnamon powder	*Salt and pepper, to taste*

Soak ½ onions and wheat in water about 1 hour; drain. Mash Kibbi meat with bulgur wheat mixture; add all spice, salt and pepper, to taste. Place ½ half mixture into lightly greased baking pan. Reserve other half mixture. Brown ground meat; add remaining onion, and cinnamon. Add salt and pepper, to taste. Add this layer to next layer. Top with remaining Kibbi mixture. Chill. Cut into squares and serve cold or bake at 350° F. for about 30 minutes and serve warm.

Variation: Take a rounded teaspoon of Kibbi mixture and form into football shape. Then press hole into center and add about ½ teaspoon of mixture and form around mixture to reshape football. May be served in this form cold or deep fat fried at 375° F. until lightly browned, serve warm. Yield: about 6 dozen this size. Dot Smith.

Yield: about 48 1½ '' squares   *CEDAR GROCERY LTD.*
                                                    Lafayette, La.

CHERRY TOMATO SOUFFLE

2 pt. cherry tomatoes
2 T. butter
2 T. flour
¾ c. Half and Half cream
3 lg. egg whites

¼ t. powdered mustard
2 oz. sharp cheddar, grated
2 scallion top, minced
Salt and pepper, to taste

Slice top from tomatoes and scoop out with small melon baller. Sprinkle inside tomatoes with salt and pepper. Drain upside down on paper towels. Heat flour and butter to make a paste; stir until bubbly. Stir in milk until thickened. Stir in mustard, cheese and scallions. Stir constantly until cheese melts, DO NOT BOIL. Preheat oven to 400° F. Place tomatoes in greased baking pan. Beat egg whites until stiff. Fold into cheese mixture. Spoon mixture into tomatoes, about 1 table-spoonful in each. Bake 10 to 12 minutes or until filling is golden brown. Serve immediately.

Yield: about 2 dozen

Becky Karavatakis
Lafayette, La.

BACON DUMPLINGS
SPECKKNODEL

8 thick slices bacon
3 T. onion, chopped fine
3½ c. soft bread crumbs
2 lg. eggs, beaten with
  ¼ c. Half and Half cream

½ c. flour
2 T. parsley, chopped
¼ t. dried marjoram
Dash salt and white pepper

Cook bacon in skillet until slightly crisp. Remove; saute onion in drippings until soft. Remove; saute bread crumbs in drippings until golden. Combine bread with egg mixture. Stir in flour, salt and pepper. Cover; let stand about 15 minutes. Add parsley, onion and marjoram to bacon. Shape bread mixture into 1¼'' balls and punch in center with thumb. Put about ½ rounded teaspoon bacon mixture in center and reform into balls. Cook dumplings uncovered in simmering water in large pot until moist and tender, about 3 minutes. Remove with slotted spoon. Drain. Serve warm.

Yield: 3 to 4 dozen

Becky Karavatakis
Lafayette, La.

STUFFED MUSHROOMS I

12 whole large fresh mushrooms
2 t. minced onion
1 T. butter
1 10-oz. pkg. frozen chopped
   spinach, cooked and drained

½ t. salt
⅛ t. white pepper
2 T. Parmesan cheese
2 T. butter

Clean mushrooms. Remove stems and chop fine. Saute stems with onion in 1 tablespoon butter until soft. Add chopped spinach, salt and pepper. Cook until spinach is dry, stirring constantly. Remove from heat. Stir in Parmesan cheese. Arrange mushroom caps in skillet with 2 tablespoons melted butter. Saute caps; drain and let cool. Mound one teaspoon of spinach mixture on each mushroom cap. Arrange caps in a casserole dish. Bake at 350° F. for 20 minutes. Or if you prefer, mound one teaspoon of spinach mixture on each mushroom cap and arrange in skillet with 2 tablespoon melted butter. Saute on top of stove for 2 minutes. Bake at 350° F. for 20 minutes.

Note: For party size servings, use smaller mushrooms and fill through large opening in pastry bag. R.B.K.

Yield: 12 large or 24-30 small

Becky Karavatakis
Lafayette, La.

STUFFED MUSHROOMS II

8 oz. mushrooms
¼ c. unsalted butter
4 lg. green onions, chopped
½ t. garlic salt or powder
¼ t. dry mustard
¼ t. soy sauce

⅛ t. oregano
1½ T. Parmesan
cheese, grated
1½ T. Romano
cheese, grated
2 T. Italian bread crumbs

Rinse mushrooms and remove stems. Finely chop about ½ of the mushroom stems. Mix all of remaining ingredients with chopped stems. Stuff mushroom caps with mixture. Microwave on high about 3 minutes or bake in 350° F. about 5 minutes. This entire recipe may be done in the food processor.

Yield: 3 to 4 dozen

Unna P. Kukla
Houston, Texas

STUFFED MUSHROOMS III

2 T. butter
1 med. onion, minced
¼ c. green pepper, minced
1 clove garlic, minced
1 lb. stemmed mushrooms

½ c. fine diced pepperoni
3 T. Parmesan cheese, grated
12 crackers, crushed
¼ t. oregano
⅓ c. chicken broth

Saute onion, pepper, and garlic in butter until limp. Add pepperoni, cheese, crackers, and oregano. Mix well. Add broth to moisten. Fill mushroom with 1 tablespoonful mixture and place in baking dish. Carefully pour water to depth of ¼" in dish with mushrooms. Bake at 325° F. for 25 minutes. Serve warm.

Yield: about 2 dozen

Alice Eastin
Lafayette, La.

MUSHROOMS LIVERWURST

1 lb. mushrooms (24/lb)	2 T. Bleu cheese dressing
4 T. butter	1 T. onion, minced
4 oz. liverwurst,	¼ t. salt
roll type	3 T. Italian bread crumbs
1 T. Worcestershire	2 T. Parmesan cheese, grated

Wash and stem mushrooms. Saute mushrooms in butter about 5 minutes. Drain. Blend liverwurst, dressing, onion and salt. Stuff into mushrooms. Top with cheese and bread crumbs. Broil 4 to 5 inches from heat for 3 to 5 minutes. Serve warm.

Yield: 24

SARMADES
PORK STUFFED CABBAGE LEAVES

1½ lb. lean pork,	½ t. dried mint
course ground	Salt and pepper
2 onions, minced	2 cabbages
¼ c. olive oil	Avgolemono Sauce (p.23)
½ c. raw rice	

Saute pork and onions in oil until browned. Add rice, mint, salt and pepper. Separate and parboil cabbage leaves. Remove center vein and divide in half. Place one tablespoon of filling near end; fold over edges and roll up. Place extra cabbage leaves on bottom of greased pot. Place sarmades in pot and cover with water. Weigh down with inverted plate and cook over very low heat for 1½ hours, adding a little water as needed. Serve with Avgolemono Sauce.

Yield: 3 to 5 dozen

Becky Karavatakis
Lafayette, La.

DOLMADAKIA
STUFFED GRAPE LEAVES

4 med. onions, chopped fine
⅔ c. raw rice
¾ c. olive oil
½ c. parsley, chopped

Juice of 1 lemon
12 oz. jar grape leaves
2 c. chicken stock
1 t. fresh mint, chopped
Avgolemono Sauce (p.23)

Combine onion with rice, oil, parsley and mint. Wash grape leaves thoroughly. Remove stem portion which extends past leaves. Place 1 teaspoon of mixture on leaf; fold the sides over and roll forward. Continue until finished. Spread remaining leaves across the bottom of a greased sauce pot. Carefully place the stuffed grape leaves, to fill one layer at a time, until all are in the pot, leaving any vacant area to the middle. If any filling is left, spoon into the center area. Place a heavy plate on top of leaves and pour the chicken stock over the leaves. Liquid should barely cover the plate. If it does not, add enough water to cover. Bring to boil, cover, and reduce to simmer for 20 minutes, adding a little water if necessary. Serve warm or chilled, plain or with Avgolemono Sauce.

Yield: about 40

Helen Karavatakis
Skopelos, Greece

FLOUNDER IN GRAPE LEAVES

1½ lb. flounder fillets
cut into ¾'' x 1½''
1 c. olive oil
Juice of 2 lemons
1 lb. jar grape leaves,
rinsed and drained

1 t. basil
½ t. oregano
1 sm. jar capers
2 T. fresh parsley, minced
1 T. chives, minced

Remove grape leaves from jar and rinse well. Rub oil in bottom of rice pot. Place leaves flat in pot. Add 1 cup water and turn on (or boil on low on stovetop 20 minutes). Remove, drain and let cool. Mix oil, lemons, basil, oregano, parsley and chives; pour over flounder. Refrigerate about an hour. Place two pieces of flounder on each leaf. Place a caper between layers of fish. Fold sides over and roll up. Place on hot grill. Baste and turn often. Remove when fish is firm, about 5 minutes on each side.

Variation: Place leftover leaves in bottom of greased rice pot. Carefully place stuffed rolls next to each other one layer at a time; add ½ c. water and remaining marinade, and turn on.

Yield: about 4 dozen

Becky Karavatakis
Lafayette, La.

L'ESCARGOT ROYAL

2 cans snails (18)
1 clove garlic
1 bay leaf
1 T. celery, minced
1 T. dry parsley
¾ c. butter

¼ c. white wine
1 c. chicken broth
2 T. green onion tops
minced
¼ t. salt
⅛ t. white pepper

Rinse snails and place in sauce pan with garlic and bay leaf. Add wine and broth. Bring to boil; reduce heat and simmer 3 to 5 minutes. Drain and wash. Place in shells or small baking dish. Heat butter with celery, parsley, onion, salt and pepper. Pour over snails and bake at 350° F. for 5 minutes. Serve warm.

Yield: 36

L'ESCARGOT IN STRAWBERRY SAUCE

2 cans snails (18)
10 oz. frozen strawberries
1 t. cornstarch
1 T. lemon juice
¼ c. butter

1 c. chicken broth
½ c. brandy
¼ t. salt
1 rib celery, halved

Rinse snails and place in sauce pan with celery and salt. Add ¼ cup brandy and broth. Bring to boil; reduce heat and simmer 3 to 5 minutes. Drain and wash. Place in shells or baking dish. Rinse and hull strawberries. Run through blender. Puree. Add cornstarch and lemon juice. Blend. Pour into sauce pan and bring to boil. Cook, stirring constantly, until slightly thickened. Remove from heat and stir in remaining ¼ c. brandy. Pour over snails and bake at 350° F. for 5 minutes. Serve warm.

Yield: 36

Becky Karavatakis
Lafayette, La.

DESSERTS

PLUM DUMPLINGS
ZWETSCHKENKNODEL

1½ lbs. sm. Italian plums
2 c. milk
2 T. butter
¾ c. flour

2 lg. eggs
Pinch of salt
3 oz. butter
3 oz. bread crumbs

Put milk and 2 tablespoons butter into saucepan and bring to boil. Add flour, reduce heat and stir with wooden spoon until pastry comes away from sides and forms a ball. Stir in eggs, one at a time, mixing well after each addition. Let cool. Turn onto well floured board and form into long sausage shape roll. Slice off enough to wrap completely around each plum. Drop the "balls" into a large pot of slightly salted, boiling water. Move gently to avoid sticking. When dumplings are done they will rise to the top, then they need only to stay a minute or two more. After draining, gently roll in bread crumbs and butter. Serve with sugar.

Variation: For small bite size portions, try seedless red grapes. Also, instead of bread crumbs, butter and sugar, try butter and graham crackers. This size yields 3 to 4 dozen. R.B.K.

Yield: 18 to 20

Sandy Shoemaker Natterer
Charlottesville, Virginia

BAKLAVA

1 lb. pecans, chopped
½ lb. walnuts, chopped
½ lb. almonds, chopped
1 lb. phyllo leaves
¾ c. sugar

½ lb. butter, melted
Dash ground cloves
1 T. cinnamon
Syrup

Combine nuts, sugar and cinnamon. Butter 12x18x1″ sheet pan. Line bottom with one sheet of phyllo. Butter and continue adding sheets and buttering until 10 buttered sheets are stacked in the bottom of the pan. Divide the nut mixture into thirds. Sprinkle ⅓ mixture on buttered phyllo sheets. Cover with 2 more buttered sheets. Repeat procedure for second ⅓ of mixture. Add final ⅓ mixture and top with 8 buttered sheets of phyllo. With a sharp knife, score through the upper two layers. Brush melted butter between the scoring and around the edges of the pan. Bake at 300° F. for about 1 hour or until golden in color. Cool. Pour hot syrup over the baklava. Cut through into about 1¼″ square or use Greek traditional cut, cross-cut at angle to create diamond shape.

Syrup
¾ c. sugar
¾ c. honey
2 c. water

1 3″ stick cinnamon, whole
Juice of ½ lemon
2-3 whole cloves

Bring to boil, reduce to medium-low heat and boil for 20 minutes. Strain. Pour hot syrup over cool baklava.

Yield: 8 to 10 dozen

Becky Karavatakis
Lafayette, La.

CHEESE STRUDLES

8 oz. cream cheese
1 T. melted butter
1½ c. shredded Swiss cheese
1 stick melted butter

1 t. vanilla
2 T. brown sugar
16 phyllo leaves

Combine 1 tablespoon melted butter with cheeses, vanilla and brown sugar. Unroll phyllo leaves. Remove 4 leaves and cover remaining leaves. One at a time brush 4 leaves with melted butter and stack together. On the short end of the stack, spread ¼ of mixture and roll tightly, like a jellyroll. Butter the top and score with a sharp knife about ¼" deep at 1" intervals at about 45 degree angle beginning at one end. Repeat to make 4 rolls. Wrap each in plastic wrap and freeze in airtight container. Bake at 400° F. on ungreased baking sheet for 15 to 20 minutes, or until golden. Cool. Cut on markings into serving pieces.

Yield: 4 dozen

Becky Karavatakis
Lafayette, La.

BEIGNETS
NEW ORLEANS DOUGHNUTS

1 ¼ c. boiling water

¼ c. Crisco

⅓ c. sugar

7 to 7½ c. flour

1 t. sugar

1 pkg. dry yeast

¼ c. warm water (110° F.)

2 lg. eggs, beaten

1 t. salt

Powdered sugar

Dissolve yeast in ¼ c. warm water with 1 teaspoon sugar. Pour boiling water over Crisco; stir in ⅓ cup sugar and salt. Add milk; stir in yeast mixture and eggs. Beat in 2 cups of flour. Add enough additional flour to make a soft dough. Put in greased bowl and turn to grease sides. Cover with slightly damp cloth and heavy plate. Refrigerate until ready to use. Roll out on lightly floured board to ⅛" thick. Cut into 1½" squares. Put thermometer in oil and heat to 360 ° F. Fry 3 to 4 at a time turning only once until golden. Drain on paper towels; immediately sprinkle tops with powdered sugar. Serve hot. If you are not going to cook all at once, return unused portion to refrigerator.

Yield: 7 to 8 dozen

Becky Karavatakis
Lafayette, La.

DOUGHNUTS

2 lg. eggs

¾ c. sugar

1 c. sour cream

2 T. butter, melted

2½ c. flour

Peanut oil for frying

2 t. baking powder

1 t. baking soda

½ t. salt

½ t. ground nutmeg

¼ t. mace

Cinnamon sugar

Sift together flour, baking powder, soda, salt, nutmeg and mace; reserve. Beat eggs; continue beating and slowly add sugar. Beat in sour cream and butter. Stir in flour mixture. Cover and refrigerate about ½ hour. Roll dough on floured board to about ¼″ thick. Cut with mini doughnut cutter (or small 1¼″ cutter). Cover with towel on board and let stand about 10 minutes. Heat peanut oil about 3 inches deep to 375° F. Fry doughnuts 3 to 4 at a time turning once until golden brown. Drain on paper towels. Sprinkle with cinnamon sugar if desired.

Variations: 1) use 1½ c. whole wheat flour and 1 cup flour; 2) cut without hole in middle; fill with favorite filling or top with chocolate.

Yield: 6 to 7 dozen

Becky Karavatakis
Lafayette, La.

MINI CHEESECAKES

½ c. graham cracker crumbs
2 T. butter, melted
8 oz. pkg. cream cheese
  softened
Lemon Curd

¼ c. sugar
1 lg. egg
½ t. vanilla extract
24 Cream Cheese Pastry
Shells (p. 60)

Combine graham cracker crumbs and butter, mixing well. Grease mini muffin tins. Spoon 1 teaspoon graham cracker mixture into each and press evenly into bottom. Beat cheese until fluffy. Add sugar and mix well. Add egg and vanilla and beat again until smooth. Spoon over graham crackers. Bake at 350° F. for about 10 minutes. Spoon about 1 teaspoon Lemon Curd over each cheesecake. Chill about one hour.

Variation: Try strawberry, cherry or grape preserves.

Lemon Curd
3 lg. eggs
2 lg. egg yolks
1 c. sugar
1 stick butter, softened

1½ T. lemon peel,
fine grated
½ c. lemon juice

Beat eggs with egg yolks. Continue beating over low fire or double boiler while slowly adding sugar. Briskly stir in lemon juice, and lemon peel. Stir constantly and continue cooking for 5 minutes. Add butter and continue stirring until thick and creamy (about 20 minutes). Store in airtight jar in refrigerator for up to 3 weeks. Makes 1 pint.

Yield: 2 dozen

Becky Karavatakis
Lafayette, La.

ROSETTES

2 lg. eggs
1 c. milk
1 c. flour
1 T. sugar

1 t. vanilla extract
⅛ t. salt
1 qt. peanut oil
Powdered sugar

Beat eggs. Add milk, flour, sugar, extract, and salt. Beat until smooth. Heat oil to 375° F. Heat rosette iron in hot oil; drain on paper toweling. Dip iron into batter until mold is about ⅔ covered and then directly into hot oil. Cook rosettes about 30 to 40 seconds, remove from iron and drain on paper towels. Dust with powdered sugar.

Yield: about 4 dozen 2" diameter

Becky Karavatakis
Lafayette, La.

RUGELACH I

1 c. butter
2 c. flour
1 lg. egg yolk
¾ c. sour cream

¾ c. sugar
1 t. cinnamon
¾ c. pecans, chopped
fine

Cut butter into flour in processor. Add egg yolk and sour cream. Process to form a ball. Remove; wrap in plastic wrap and refrigerate overnight. Combine sugar, cinnamon and pecans. Divide dough into 4 equal portions. Roll each on floured board to 8" circle. Sprinkle ¼ of the filling on each circle. Use pizza wheel and divide into 16 wedges. Roll each from widest to smallest, slightly curling ends to form a crescent shape. Repeat with remaining dough and filling. Bake on greased cookie sheet at 375° F. until light brown, about 12 minutes. Can be frozen before or after baking.

Yield: 64

Leslie Henfield
Baton Rouge, La.

RUGELACH II

8 oz. pkg. cream cheese
1 c. butter, room temp.

2 t. vanilla
2 c. flour

Mix cream cheese, butter and vanilla until smooth. Add flour and mix until dough begins to cling together in a ball. Cover and refrigerate several hours or overnight.

Filling:
½ c. sugar
1 c. fine chopped nuts

2¼ T. cinnamon
1½ T. butter
Powdered sugar

Combine and set aside.

Preheat oven to 375° F. Divide dough into 4 equal portions. On floured board, roll dough into 8 inch circles. Spread each portion with ¼ of nut filling. Cut each circle into 16 equal wedges. Roll up wedges, beginning from wide end pressing tip into dough to secure. Place seam side down on ungreased baking sheet. Bake 15 to 20 minutes or until golden. Remove cookies from sheets and cool on rack. While still warm sprinkle tops with powdered sugar.

Yield: 64

Kathleen Esteb
Baton Rouge, La.

LEMON BAVARIAN

1 c. Half and Half cream
¾ c. sugar
½ c. lemon juice
1 t. grated lemon peel
6 lg. egg yolks, beaten
1 envelope unflavored
   gelatin
¼ c. cold water

1 c. whipping cream
1 c. whipping cream,
   whipped
2 T. powdered sugar
1 t. grated lemon peel
⅓ c. pecans or walnuts,
   chopped fine
60 Cream Cheese Pastry
   Shells (p. 60)

Heat Half and Half cream, sugar, lemon juice and lemon peel over medium heat, stirring constantly to a boil. Remove from heat. Beat eggs and stir ¼ cup of lemon mixture into the eggs. Stir egg mixture into remaining lemon mixture and heat to boiling, stirring constantly. Remove from heat. Soften gelatin in ¼ cup water and stir into lemon mixture until dissolved. Stir in 1 cup whipping cream and pour into well greased mold. Refrigerate overnight. Turn out on serving tray. Mix whipped cream and powdered sugar. Pipe over top of mold from pastry bag. Sprinkle chopped nuts and grated lemon peel over top. Serve as a spread with ladyfinger cookies or prebaked shells for filling.

Yield: about 4 cups filling
for 60 mini-shells

Becky Karavatakis
Lafayette, La.

PEACH-ALMOND BITES

½ c. butter
1 lg. egg yolk
1 c. flour
36 almonds

⅓ c. sugar
¼ t. almond extract
¼ t. salt
Peach Filling

Make Peach Filling; reserve. Cream butter and sugar; stir in egg yolk and almond extract. Sift flour and salt together. Add and mix well. Shape into 3 dozen 1″ balls. Place 2 inches apart on greased baking sheet. Make a deep indention in center of each ball. Bake at 325° F. for 20 to 30 minutes. Remove to wire rack. While still warm fill centers with cooled peach filling. Brush with corn syrup and top with almond.

Peach Filling
¾ c. Ruston peaches,
   mashed
¾ c. water

⅔ c. sugar
½ t. vanilla

Place ingredients in sauce pan and cook over medium-lot heat about 30 minutes until mixture is clear and thickened.

Yield: 36

Mildred Moench Tuten
Ruston, La.

CARROT CAKE

2 c. flour
2 c. sugar
1½ c. oil
3 c. grated carrots
1½ t. soda

1 t. salt
1 c. cinnamon
4 lg. eggs
1 t. vanilla

Mix dry ingredients. Add oil. Add eggs, one at a time, blending after each addition. Add carrots. Bake at 350° F. for 45 to 50 minutes or until done. Top with frosting.

Frosting
1 stick oleo
1½ c. powdered sugar
Chopped pecans

8 oz. cream cheese
½ t. vanilla

Combine ingredients

Yield: 1 9"x13" cake
    48 1½" squares

Jo Elwell
Lafayette, La.

BANANA MINCEMEAT BREAD

2 c. unbleached flour
½ c. whole wheat flour
1 T. baking soda
1 t. salt
2 c. sugar
1 c. butter
4 lg. eggs

2½ c. bananas, mashed
1 c. mincemeat
½ c. macadamia nuts,
chopped coarsely
2 T. powdered sugar
2 T. macadamia nuts,
chopped fine

Preheat oven to 350° F. Sift flours, soda and salt. Beat sugar and butter until light. Add eggs, beating after each addition. Beat ⅓ flour mixture into sugar mixture, then ½ banana mixture, alternating until all flour mixture is added. Fold in mincemeat and ½ cup nuts. Divide batter into 2 9″x5″ loaf pans. Bake until done, about 1 to 1¼ hours. Test with pick. Cool on wire rack for 15 minutes; remove from pans. Combine powdered sugar and remaining nuts and sprinkle over loaves while slightly warm.

Variation: try Cranberry Chutney (p. 27) instead of mincemeat.

Yield: 2 loaves

Becky Karavatakis
Lafayette, La.

KOURABIEDES

1 lb. butter

3 T. powdered sugar

Powdered sugar for topping

2 lg. egg yolks

5 c. flour, sifted

Cream butter until fluffy. Beat in sugar. Beat in egg yolks and blend well. Add flour, one cup at a time until soft dough is formed. Shape into small balls or crescent shapes. Place about 1'' apart on greased cookie sheet. Preheat oven to 350° F. and bake 18 to 20 minutes or lightly browned. Sift sugar on waxed paper and place the cookies on top while still warm. Sift additional sugar over top. Let cool. Store in airtight container with powdered sugar.

Variation: Brush tops of baked cookies with small amount of orange water or rose water just before dusting with powdered sugar. H.K.

Yield: 9 to 10 dozen

Helen Karavatakis
Skopelos, Greece

LADYFINGERS

5 lg. egg yolks

1 c. scant flour, sifted

1½ T. sugar

½ c. plus 1 T. sugar

5 lg. egg whites

Powdered sugar

Beat egg yolks on medium speed. Beat in ½ cup plus 1 tablespoon sugar about 3 minutes. Fold flour into mixture. Beat egg whites to soft peaks. Add 1½ tablespoons sugar and beat until stiff. Gently fold into flour just to mix. Pipe batter from pastry bag with ½'' hole about 1½'' long on parchment-lined baking sheets. Sprinkle with powdered sugar. Bake until light brown around the edges, about 12 minutes, at 350° F. Cool on wire racks.

Yield: about 5 dozen

Becky Karavatakis
Lafayette, La.

NUTTY BUTTER BALLS

1 lb. butter
2 lbs. peanut butter
3 lbs. powdered sugar

1 c. pecans, chopped
2 lbs. semi-sweet chocolate

Melt butter and mix with peanut butter and sugar. Knead in pecans. Roll dough into ¾" balls. Set on wax paper. Melt chocolate in double boiler. Using small teaspoon or slotted candy spoon, dip balls in chocolate, coating well. Set on wax paper to cool. Allow 3 to 4 hours for coating to harden. Store in airtight container.

Yield: about 200 pieces

Alice Eastin
Lafayette, La.

DATE PECAN BALLS

1 c. soft butter
2 t. vanilla
2 c. pecans

½ c. sugar
2 c. flour
1 c. dates, cut up

Cream butter and sugar. Add vanilla and mix. Add flour and mix. Blend in pecans and dates. Roll by teaspoonful into balls. Refrigerate for 1 to 2 hours. Bake at 350° F. for about 20 minutes. Remove from oven and roll in powdered sugar. Sprinkle again with powdered sugar after cooled.

Yield: 4 to 5 dozen

Becky Bishop
Lafayette, La.

CHESS PIE SQUARES

1 box yellow cake mix
1 stick butter, softened
1 lg. egg, beaten
1 T. water

8 oz. cream cheese, softened
3 lg. eggs
1 t. vanilla
1 lb. powdered sugar

Mix cake mix together well with butter, 1 egg, and tablespoonful water. Press into well greased 9"x13" baking pan. Beat eggs, one at a time into softened cream cheese, until well blended. Add sugar and vanilla and mix well. Pour over batter and bake at 350° F. for about 45 minutes or until slightly browned and knife inserted into center comes out clean. Cool and cut into 1¼" squares.

Yield: 70

Marsha Runnels
Baton Rouge, La.

GINNY'S FRUITCAKE COOKIES

1 lb. candied cherries
2 slices candied pineapple
1 lb. dates
1 lb. pecans, chopped

1 c. sugar
1 c. flour
1 T. baking powder
4 lg. eggs

Chop fruit; dredge in flour to keep from sticking. Add pecans, sugar, flour and baking powder. Mix well; blend in eggs. Drop by teaspoon on greased cookie sheet. Bake in preheated oven at 325° F. until golden, about 15 minutes.

Yield: 6 to 7 dozen

Ginny Augsburger
Houston, Texas

PECAN PIE BARS

2 c. flour
1 c. packed brown sugar
½ c. butter
½ c. margarine
5 eggs

1 c. dark corn syrup
¾ c. sugar
1 t. vanilla
1 c. broken pecans
Dash salt

Preheat oven to 350° F. In a large mixing bowl, combine flour and brown sugar. Cut in butter and margarine with a pastry blender or two knives until mixtures resembles course crumbs. Press crumb mixture into a 9x13 pan. Bake for 10 minutes or until golden. While crust is baking, combine eggs, corn syrup, sugar, salt and vanilla; blend well. Stir in pecans. Pour filling over hot crust; reduce heat to 275° F. and bake for 50 minutes or until center is set. Cool in pan on a wire rack before cutting into bars.

Yield: 36 1"x3" bars
      or 72 1"x1½" bars

Odell Killingsworth
Lafayette, La.

PRALINE SQUARES

12 graham crackers
2 sticks oleo
1 c. lt. brown sugar

2 c. pecans or almonds,
chopped

Bring oleo and sugar to boil for 3 minutes, stirring often. Spread over graham crackers. Sprinkle tops with chopped nuts. Bake in preheated 350° F. oven for 10 minutes. Cool. Cut each graham cracker into 8 squares or 6 finger strips.

Yield: 96 squares or
      72 finger strips

Vivian Mays
Lafayette, La.

MILLIONAIRES

1 14-oz. pkg. Kraft caramels
6 to 6½ c. pecan halves
2 12-oz. pkg. chocolate
   chips

3-3½ T. water
1 4-oz. block paraffin
½ t. vanilla
Wax paper

Place caramels and water in double boiler. Melt. Stir in pecans. Drop by teaspoon on to wax paper. Put in freezer about 45 minutes. Melt paraffin with chocolate chips. Remove from heat and stir in vanilla. Return to low heat and dip cold caramels and return them to wax paper to set.

Yield: 6 to 8 dozen

Sharron Mayers
Baton Rouge, La.

PEANUT BRITTLE

(Use All Level Measurements)

1 c. peanuts
¾ c. sugar
½ c. light karo syrup

¼ c. water
1 t. baking soda

Put skillet on high heat. Add peanuts, sugar, syrup and water, stir. When it begins to bubble, reduce heat to medium. Stir occasionally. Cook 7 minutes, mixture should be pale yellow. Remove from heat and immediately add soda. Stir very fast and pour quickly onto well greased baking sheet. Let cool. Break into pieces and store in airtight container.

Variations: substitute pecans or walnuts, or omit nuts for plain brittle.

Yield: about 1 pound

Gertrude Roesler Brown
Sunset, La.

MICRO-PEANUT BRITTLE

1 c. sugar	1 t. butter
½ c. light Karo syrup	1 t. vanilla
1 c. roasted, salted peanuts	1 t. soda

Combine sugar and karo in a 1½ quart casserole; stir well. Cook in microwave on high 4 minutes. Stir in peanuts. Cook 3 to 5 minutes on high or until light brown. Add butter and vanilla to syrup, blending well. Cook 1 to 2 minutes more on high. Add soda and stir gently until light and foamy. Pour mixture onto lightly greased cookie sheet or wax paper. Cool, and break into small pieces and store in airtight container.

Variations: 1) Almond Brittle: substitute 7 ozs. dry roasted almonds and 1 t. almond extract for vanilla; 2) Pecan Brittle: substitute 1 c. pecans.

Yield: about 1 pound

Becky Karavatakis
Lafayette, La.

"TEXAS PARTY OIL"
BRANDIED CHOCOLATE SAUCE

½ c. evaporated milk	2 T. brandy
6 oz. pkg. chocolate chips	Dash salt

In a small saucepan scald milk; remove from heat. Add chocolate chips and stir until mixture is smooth. Stir in brandy and salt. Serve from chafing dish or fondue pot. Serve with assorted fresh fruit and picks for dipping.

Variation: try 6 oz. pkg. caramels instead of chocolate chips and 2 T. rum instead of brandy. R.B.K.

Yield: about 1½ cups

Rosalie Turner
Houston, Texas

KOLACHES

1½ c. flour
1 pkg. dry yeast
½ c. evaporated milk

½ c. milk
¼ c. sugar

Heat milk to warm (105-110° F). Sprinkle yeast and sugar over milk. Allow to set for 10 minutes. Stir into flour and let rise in greased bowl until double in bulk. Then add the following:

1½ c. flour
¼ c. butter

¼ c. Wesson oil
1 t. salt

Mix together well and let rise in warm place until double in bulk. Punch dough down and roll out on floured board to ¼" thick. Use a glass or cutter about 2½" round, dusted in flour to cut dough. Place on greased baking sheet, brush with butter and allow to double in bulk. Push center down with bowl of spoon or thumb and fill with rounded teaspoon of filing. Bake in preheated oven of 425° F. 10 to 12 minutes, DO NOT OVERBAKE. Remove from oven and cover pan with towel and let cool.

Variations: 1) Kolache hot rolls: omit filling, pinch off dough and bake as above; 2) sweet rolls; omit filling and top with powdered sugar while hot; 3) fruit Kolaches: fill with favorite preserve or jam; 4) for bite size portions use 1½" cutter and scant teaspoonful filling, baking 8 minutes or until golen.

Cream Cheese Filling
8 oz. pkg. cream cheese, softened
1½ c. sugar
2 egg yolks

Cream the cheese. Add sugar and egg yolks and mix well.

Yield: 32 (2½" size)
48 (1½" size)

Karen Todd
Needville, Texas

BEVERAGES

STRAWBERRY ICE

2 pts. strawberries
½ c. sugar
2 T. sugar

1 pt. Half and Half cream
2 c. chipped ice
6 sprigs fresh mint

Rinse and hull 1 pint of the berries. Slice and sprinkle with 2 tablespoons sugar. Reserve. Puree other pint of berries with cream. Add sugar and ice. Process about 30 seconds. Serve immediately from stemmed wine glasses. Top with sliced berry mixture and garnish with sprig of fresh mint.

Yield: 10 4-oz. servings

Becky Karavatakis
Lafayette, La.

SLUSHY FROZEN PUNCH

6 3-oz. pkg. lime jello
2 46-oz. cans pineapple
  juice
1 16-oz. bottle real
  lemon juice

5 c. sugar
16 c. water
2 qts. ginger ale
2-oz. bottle almond
  flavoring

Reserve ginger ale and almond flavoring. Mix remaining ingredients together until thoroughly dissolved. Divide into 2 5-quart ice cream buckets and freeze. Remove from freezer 4 hours before serving. Just before serving add ginger ale and almond flavoring; stir, it will be slushy.

Yield: 80 4-oz. cups

Eva Dell Daigre
Lafayette, La.

MINT PUNCH

5 42-oz. cans apple juice
5 42-oz. cans pineapple juice
4 6-oz. cans frozen limeade w/
  water as directed
4 6-oz. cans frozen lemonade w/
  water as directed

6 qts. ginger ale
4 c. sugar
1-oz. oil of peppermint
or to taste
Green or red food
coloring, if desired

Mix together. Chill. Freeze a portion to float in punch bowl.

Yield: about 5½ gallons
175 4-oz. servings

Eva Dell Daigre
Lafayette, La.

FRUIT PUNCH

1 46-oz. can unsweetened
  pineapple juice
1 32-oz. bottle apple juice

1 64-oz. carton orange juice
1 2 liter bottle ginger ale
1 sm. can pineapple chunks

Mix juices together. Pour 2 cups blended juices into ring mold and freeze. Reserve remaining juice in refrigerator. When ready to serve, pour juices into punch bowl, add ginger ale and float juice ring on top. Garnish with chunks of pineapple and mint leaves if desired.

Yield: 6½ quarts or
52 4-oz. servings

Becky Karavatakis
Lafayette, La.

CAJUN FRUIT PUNCH

1½ to 2 t. cinnamon　　　　　　　　　　　　*1 pt. cream*
1 pt. coffee　　　　　　　　　　　　　　*Sugar to taste*
Whipped cream

Combine cinnamon and sugar with coffee and heat. Heat cream in separate pot. Pour coffee and cream at the same time from separate pots into cup. Top with whipped cream.

Yield: 6 servings　　　　　　　　　　　　　*Alice Leblanc*
　　　　　　　　　　　　　　　　　　　　Lafayette, La.

HAWAIIAN TEA COOLER

1 c. sugar　　　　　　　　　　　　　　*2 c. strong tea*
⅔ c. orange juice　　　　　　　　　　　　*2 c. water*
2 c. pineapple juice　　　　　　　　　*1½ c. lemon juice*
4 c. ginger ale

Boil sugar and water for 5 minutes, stirring to dissolve sugar. Combine juices and tea. Let cool. Refrigerate until ready to serve. Add ginger ale just before serving.

Yield: 24 4-oz. servings　　　　　　　　*Becky Karavatakis*
　　　　　　　　　　　　　　　　　　　　Lafayette, La.

SWEDISH COFFEE NOG

6 lg. eggs, separated
1 c. sugar or substitute
5 cups strong coffee
1 T. powdered sugar
1-2 dashes salt

1 pt. Half and Half cream
1½ pts. whipping cream
1 pt. whipping cream
Fine grated orange peel

Beat egg yolks. Beat in 1 cup sugar until thick. Stir in 1½ pints whipping cream, Half and Half, coffee, and salt. Refrigerate. Beat 1 cup of whipping cream with powdered sugar until stiff. Fold into eggnog mixture. Beat egg whites until stiff. Fold into eggnog mixture. Refrigerate one hour or until ready to serve. Pour ½ mixture in punch bowl, reserve remainder for filling in refrigerator. Top each cup with a pinch of fine grated orange peel.

Yield: about 40 servings

COFFEE PUNCH

1 gal. strong coffee
½ c. sugar
1 pt. whipped cream

1 T. vanilla
1 qt. vanilla ice cream

Freeze 1 pint coffee in ring mold. Combine remaining ingredients and refrigerate until ready to serve. Serve from punch bowl with coffee ring to cool punch.

Variations: 1) omit vanilla and replace with almond extract; 2) Add ½ cup chocolate syrup and replace 1 t. vanilla with 1 t. orange or mint extract; 3) replace ice cream with eggnog, sprinkle top with nutmeg; 4) use decaf coffee, sweetener, lo-fat whipped cream and ice milk.

Yield: 42 4-oz. servings

Becky Karavatakis
Lafayette, La.

CONCORD PUNCH

2 qts. Welche's grape juice
¾ c. brown sugar
1 t. cinnamon

½ t. nutmeg
Dash of cloves
Dash of ginger

Combine in sauce pan over medium heat. Bring to boil; reduce to simmer. Serve warm.

Yield: 16 4-oz. portions

MULLED CIDER

2 qts. apple cider
1½ c. sugar
6 broken cinnamon sticks

15 whole cloves
12 whole allspice
Cinnamon sticks

Combine cider, sugar, 6 cinnamon sticks, cloves and allspice over low heat, stirring occasionally, until sugar is dissolved. DO NOT BOIL. Remove from heat and let stand 2 to 3 hours. Strain and refrigerate until ready to serve. Heat just until hot. Garnish with cinnamon sticks.

Variation: try 1 quart each, apple and white grape or apple and cranberry.

Yield: about 2 quarts

Becky Karavatakis
Lafayette, La.

HOT MULLED PUNCH

48-oz. bottle cranberry juice
2 qt. bottles apple juice
½ c. brown sugar

½ t. salt
4 cinnamon sticks
1 ½ t. whole cloves

Pour cranberry and apple juice in pot. Add brown sugar and salt. Stir until sugar is dissolved. Tie cinnamon and cloves in cheese cloth and place into pot. Cover and place on very low heat for 2 hours. Remove spice bag. Serve warm.

Yield: 20 4-oz. servings

Carol Christie
Lafayette, La.

CRANBERRY TEA

2 sticks cinnamon
1 c. sugar
2 6-oz. cans frozen
   pink lemonade
2 46-oz. cans apple juice

1 quart water
2 #2 cans cranberry sauce
Add water as instructed w/
lemonade

Simmer cinnamon in 1 quart water 30 to 40 minutes until liquid is reduced to 2 cups. Remove cinnamon. Dissolve sugar and cranberry sauce in the hot liquid. Add pink lemonade and water as directed on cans and apple juice. Mix well. Heat before serving, but Do Not Boil.

Yield: 30 6-oz. servings

Eva Dell Daigre
Lafayette, La.

"SALAD BAR" STYLE PUNCH

Base:
2 pt. plain yogurt
23 oz. bottle Perrier water

Chill well. Blend together. Make as much as you wish; however, it is better to mix one batch at a time.

Mixers:
6 oz. can frozen Strawberry Daiquiri mixer
6 oz. can frozen Pina Colada mixer
6 oz. can frozen Mai Tai Punch mixer

Note: you may use any 6 oz. frozen concentrate juice or mixer- lemonade, grape juice, apple juice, orange juice, etc.

Let thaw and serve from individual bowls with spoon.

Spiked:
6 oz. light rum
6 oz. vodka
6 oz. gin

Serve from small pitchers or as with mixers.

Garnishes:
Stemmed cherries
Pineapple chunks
Lemon slices
Lime slices
Orange slices
Mint sprigs

Arrange in divided dishes with toothpicks.

Serve plain for those on diets or blend in favorite mixers and to with choice of garnishes.

Yield: 11 5-oz. servings

Becky Karavatakis
Lafayette, La.

LAGNIAPPE

RECYCLING LEFTOVERS

When it comes to making Hors d'oeuvres, just about anything goes. Leftovers are perfect for making those tiny mouth-watering tidbits. Just be sure that you use the "leftovers" quickly to preserve their quality.

Phyllo
Phyllo is sold in one pound packages, which contain 28 to 30 sheets about 12 by 16 inches in size. Properly wrapped they can remain fresh in the refrigerator about 2 weeks. Cut into 2" strips, with pizza wheel cutting entire depth of pastry. Excellent way to use up the rest of your Crawfish Etouffee, Shrimp Creole, Oyster Dressing, or your Broccoli Casserole! Just about any meat, vegetable or dessert filling can be used. The ends of several cheeses can be combined with a little butter, and egg and some seasonings for a delightful filling. After all, these tiny pitas (pies) require only 1 teaspoon of filling, placed at the end of the buttered strip and folded over like folding "OLD GLORY." They may even be frozen while phyllo is still raw. Freeze in single layers in airtight containers. These may be kept in the freezer from 2 to 6 weeks depending upon the choice of filling — so be sure to date your packages.

Spreads, Dips and Fillings
Leftover meats can be put into the processor with various items and ground to make excellent spreads for tiny sandwiches or fillings for puff shells, or tart shells. They can be thinned with sour cream or cream cheese to create dips. Vegetables, such as broccoli work well with cheese and onions, perhaps and mushroom soup. Meats can be frozen, wrapped tightly and thawed just before mixing. Remember — DO NOT FREEZE if they contain mayonnaise, sour cream, gelatin or boiled egg whites.

Egg Roll or Won Ton Wraps
Leftover taco meat — saute a little chopped onion and celery with a little shredded cabbage in peanut and sesame oil. Stir in taco meat, For mini-egg rolls use Won Ton wraps and place a small amount in center, brush edges with water, and fold over opposite corners. Roll up and seal. Freeze as above for up to 2 weeks. Deep fry at 375 degrees until golden. Serve with choice of sauces. This works equally well with shrimp, chicken, or leftover turkey stir-fried with shredded potatoes and carrots.

Plan Ahead

If you know you will be working on party foods, plan the amount you cook to include enough to serve a regular meal to the family with plenty left for party foods. This way you save time and you don't have any waste.

Making biscuits for breakfast? Make a double batch and make some mini-size. Freeze these before baking for up to 8 weeks. Same with tart shells. Next time you make a pie shell — make two batches, cut one batch with 2" daisy or round cookie cutter and line mini-muffin pans. Prick bottoms and bake for easy filling of pre-cooked goodies or freeze raw for baking just prior to use. Leftover pie dough can sit for 3 to 4 days in refrigerator and be rolled out to make meat pies, and such and frozen 2 to 6 weeks as well. Making bread — make a little extra and bake in party size pans or make such with triple folded foil. Freeze whole and remove the morning of use. Unwrap, slice, let thaw and then wrap again until ready to use.

"TOOLS OF THE TRADE"

My single most important tool is my imagination, let that be also yours. There are hundreds of pans and tools that can be used. These are just as few of the ones I find most useful.

An Empty Frozen Juice Can
Cut in half. Use needle nosed pliers and bend cut end to desired special shape.

#100 Spring Release, Ice Cream Scoop
Use this to make uniform meatballs, mini-cream puffs, anything which requires a teaspoonful or round shape.

#70 Spring Release, Ice Cream Scoop
As above but holds a tablespoonful.

2" Daisy Shaped Cookie Cutter
Perfect for cutting out pastries to line mini-muffin pans, for bite-size pastries.

Mini-Muffin Pans or Mini-Tart Pans
Perfect for bite-size pastries.

#4-S Styrofoam Meat Trays
Can be purchased from local butchers. Perfect for freezing Hors d'Oeuvres. (Fits inside gallon size Zip-Loc Freezer bag and makes protecting and stacking easy.)

Various Sized Melon Ballers
Perfect for fruit bowls and fruit kabobs used for decorations. (Carrots, potatoes and other vegetables are great stir-fried in peanut oil with dash of sesame oil, served with dipping sauce.)

Canelle Knife or Lemon Stripper
Great for garnishes from any citrus fruits and many vegetables.

Butter Curler
A hooked shaped gadget great for making butter or cream cheese curls. (Form 24 oz. cream cheese to cone shape. Chill. Carefully rake curls from top to bottom about 1 inch long. Makes pretty Christmas tree. Sprinkle with crushed parsley.)

Garnishing Knife
A French knife used to make krinkle or waffle cuts. Great for carrots and beets for vegetable platters.

Twin Curl Cutter
A German tool used to create vegetables and fruit curls of contrasting colors. (Also great for stir-frying carrots and potatoes together.)

Spiral Slicer
An American tool used to turn vegetables into beautiful ribbon. Also try flutting the edges before turning.

Small Blade Paring Knife
A great tool to use with your imagination for carving and designing.

"....THESE ARE A 'FEW' OF MY FAVORITE THINGS..."

for quick reference to all your favorite party foods

PICKLES/RELISHES

NAME OF RECIPE	*NO. OF SERVINGS*	*BOOK OR SOURCE*	*PAGE NO.*

SAUCES/JELLIES

NAME OF RECIPE	*NO. OF SERVINGS*	*BOOK OR SOURCE*	*PAGE NO.*

SOUPS/SALADS

NAME OF RECIPE	NO. OF SERVINGS	BOOK OR SOURCE	PAGE NO.

CRACKERS/BREADS

NAME OF RECIPE	NO. OF SERVINGS	BOOK OR SOURCE	PAGE NO.

PASTRIES/FILLINGS

NAME OF RECIPE	NO. OF SERVINGS	BOOK OR SOURCE	PAGE NO.

SANDWICHES/CANAPES

NAME OF RECIPE	NO. OF SERVINGS	BOOK OR SOURCE	PAGE NO.

MOLDS/SPREADS

NAME OF RECIPE	NO. OF SERVINGS	BOOK OR SOURCE	PAGE NO.

COLD DIPS

NAME OF RECIPE	NO. OF SERVINGS	BOOK OR SOURCE	PAGE NO.

HOT DIPS

NAME OF RECIPE	NO. OF SERVINGS	BOOK OR SOURCE	PAGE NO.

COLD HORS d'OEUVRES

NAME OF RECIPE	NO. OF SERVINGS	BOOK OR SOURCE	PAGE NO.

HOT HORS d'OEUVRES

NAME OF RECIPE	NO. OF SERVINGS	BOOK OR SOURCE	PAGE NO.

DESSERTS

NAME OF RECIPE	NO. OF SERVINGS	BOOK OR SOURCE	PAGE NO.

BEVERAGES

NAME OF RECIPE	NO. OF SERVINGS	BOOK OR SOURCE	PAGE NO.

MISCELLANEOUS

NAME OF RECIPE	NO. OF SERVINGS	BOOK OR SOURCE	PAGE NO.

INDEX

AROUND THE WORLD — ONE BITE AT A TIME
Available Direct From
PELIGATOR PUBLICATIONS
P.O. Box 30631   Lafayette, La. 70593-0631

La. Residents: 1st copy: @ $15.98
                                 tax   1.12
                    postage/handling   2.40
                            total   @ $19.50   _____

_____ Additional copies: @ $15.98
                                 tax   1.12
                    postage/handling   .40
                            total   @ $17.50   _____

Out-of State: 1st copy: @ $15.98
                    postage/handling   2.40
                            total   @ $18.38   _____

_____ Additional copies: @ $15.98
                    postage/handling   .40
                            total   @ $16.38   _____

Enclosed is my ____check ____money order for   _____

Please make checks payable to **PELICATOR PUBLICATIONS.** Sorry, NO C.O.D.'s, credit cards, or currency accepted.

NAME _____

ADDRESS _____

CITY _____ STATE_____ ZIP CODE_____

AROUND THE WORLD — ONE BITE AT A TIME
Available Direct From
PELIGATOR PUBLICATIONS
P.O. Box 30631   Lafayette, La. 70593-0631

La. Residents: 1st copy: @ $15.98
                                 tax   1.12
                    postage/handling   2.40
                            total   @ $19.50   _____

_____ Additional copies: @ $15.98
                                 tax   1.12
                    postage/handling   .40
                            total   @ $17.50   _____

Out-of State: 1st copy: @ $15.98
                    postage/handling   2.40
                            total   @ $18.38   _____

_____ Additional copies: @ $15.98
                    postage/handling   .40
                            total   @ $16.38   _____

Enclosed is my ____check ____money order for   _____

Please make checks payable to **PELICATOR PUBLICATIONS.** Sorry, NO C.O.D.'s, credit cards, or currency accepted.

NAME _____

ADDRESS _____

CITY _____ STATE_____ ZIP CODE_____

LOUISIANA PRODUCTS

Some of the ingredients listed below may not be known to people outside this area. If not available in your area, you may get them direct from our local factories.

TABASCO SAUCE—Tabasco Pepper Sauce, a very hot pepper sauce made from a Tabasco pepper (red pepper), vinegar and salt; curried in oak barrels. Available from McIlhenny Co., Avery Island, La. 70513.

LOUISIANA HOT SAUCE—a hot pepper sauce. Available from Bruce Food Corp., New Iberia, La. 70561.

TONY'S SEASONING—Tony Chachere's famous Creole Seasoning, a blend of salt, red pepper, garlic and other spices. Available from Creole Foods, Division of Cajun Country Cookbook, Inc., Opelousas, La. 70570.

CREOLE MUSTARD—a spicy blend of mustard. Available from Zatarain's, Inc., New Orleans, La. 70114.

TRAPPEY'S RED BEANS—with slab bacon and with or without jalapeno peppers. Available from B.F. Trappey's Sons, Inc., Lafayette, La. 70501.

CRAWFISH or MUDBUGS—Crayfish, raised all over South Louisiana.

LOUISIANA YAMS—extra dark, iron rich, sweet potatoes grown in Louisiana.

CREOLE CREAM CHEESE—a blend of 7 ounces cream cheese with 1 ounce heavy cream. No longer produced commercially.